FIRST AROUND THE WORLD
A Journal of Magellan's Voyage

FERDINAND MAGELLANUS.

GEORGE SANDERLIN

FIRST

AROUND

THE

WORLD

A JOURNAL OF MAGELLAN'S VOYAGE

HAMISH HAMILTON

First Published in Great Britain, 1966
by Hamish Hamilton Ltd.
90 Great Russell Street, London, W.C.1.
Text Copyright © 1964 by George Sanderlin

TO JOHNNY

PRINTED PHOTOLITHO IN GREAT BRITAIN
BY EBENEZER BAYLIS AND SON, LTD.
THE TRINITY PRESS, WORCESTER, AND LONDON

AUTHOR'S NOTE

Most of this book consists of selected portions of Antonio Pigafetta's *First Voyage Around the World*, as translated by J. A. Robertson. Omission of some of Pigafetta's words within a sentence is indicated by three dots; omission of a sentence or more from Pigafetta is indicated by four dots. In a few places Pigafetta's sentences are transposed so that the order of events will be clearer.

Modern place names are used instead of archaic place names (e.g., "Brazil" for Pigafetta's "Verzin"), and names of persons are given in their English or Spanish forms rather than in the Italian or Portuguese forms often used by Pigafetta. Pigafetta's Italian or Spanish units of measurement (e.g., a *braza*) are changed to English units (feet or yards).

Words inserted by the translator, Robertson, to make his version clear and enclosed by him in brackets are not bracketed here. Words inserted by the present editor for additional information (e.g., "1521" after a date given by Pigafetta) are bracketed. Words inserted by the present editor in place of a word or phrase of Pigafetta's are bracketed. Pigafetta's punctuation and capitalization are, for the most part, retained, but the paragraphing is the present editor's.

G.S.

CONTENTS

Author's Note   v

Introduction   xi

1. A New Route to the East   1

2. Across the Atlantic   25

3. Mutiny at St. Julian   51

4. The Strait of Magellan   73

5. The Cross in the Philippines   99

6. "So Noble a Captain"   125

7. The Spice Islands   141

8. Around the World   163

Index   185

MAPS AND ILLUSTRATIONS

A drawing of Lisbon Harbour in the
early 16th century (From De Bry's
Americae III, 1592)   xxiv-xxv

Globe made by Martin Behaim (1492)   10

Globe made by Johann Schöner (1515)   11

Sailing ships in the Atlantic encounter
a shoal of flying fish (From De Bry's
Americae III, 1592)   34, 35

The route of the voyage around the world   44

The Straits of Magellan today   61

An artist's impression of the discovery
of the Straits of Magellan   84-85

Map of the Philippines and the Spice Islands 103

A parrot of the Philippines   116

The death of Magellan at the battle of
Mactan, 1521 (From De Bry's
Americae IX, 1602)   134-5

Magellan's men arrive at the Moluccas
(From De Bry's *Americae V*, 1595) 152-153

The Emperor Charles V in 1520   169

ACKNOWLEDGEMENTS

The author and publishers would like to thank the following for permission to reprint copyright material in this book:

The Hispanic Society of America for the extract from *The Lusiads of Luiz de Camões*, translated by Leonard Baron; Northwestern University Press for the extracts from *Magellan's Voyage Around The World*, edited by Charles E. Nowell; The Viking Press Inc. for the extracts from *Conqueror of the Seas* by Stefan Zweig, translated by Eden and Cedar Paul; The Hakluyt Society for the extracts from *The First Voyage Around the World by Magellan*, edited by Lord Stanley of Alderley, and Thomas Y. Crowell & Co. for the extracts from *So Noble a Captain* by Charles McKew Parr.

The author and publishers would also like to thank the following for permission to reproduce the illustrations used in this book:

The National Maritime Museum for the illustrations on pages xxiv, 34, 134, and 152; The Mansell Collection for the illustration on page 116; The Royal Geographical Society for the illustration on page 61, and The Radio Times Hulton Picture Library for the illustration on page 84.

INTRODUCTION

How does one go around the world? How far is it? How long would it take?

Are there islands, monsters, or people in the South Pacific? Does South America connect with the Antarctic continent? What stars can you see near the South Pole?

Four and a half centuries ago no one knew the answers to these questions or to many others like them. But one day early in 1518, in the little Spanish hill city of Valladolid, an interview was being held which was to lead to the answers—to an epic event and a great increase in man's knowledge of the earth.

The interview was between a pale, red-haired youth who was Charles I, king of Spain, and a Portuguese navigator out of favour in his own country—Ferdinand Magellan.

Magellan, one of the bystanders commented, "was not of imposing presence, since he was small in stature and did not appear to be much." However, something about this earnest veteran of battle and shipwreck attracted the young king. Charles, who had been brought up in Flanders, waved his interpreter aside and conversed directly with Magellan in halting Spanish.

"I will discover a new route to the East by sailing west," declared the thirty-eight-year-old navigator.

Important people like the swarthy, scheming Bishop Fonseca, head of the Supreme Council of the Indies, and Cristóbal de Haro, one of the wealthiest men of his day, listened intently. To reach the East by sailing west had been Columbus's dream twenty-six years earlier, but the New World had blocked his way.

"Here," said Magellan, bringing out a hand-painted globe made of beautifully tooled leather. "Here are the Moluccas, or Spice Islands."

He pointed to a small group of islands in the midst of the East Indies, extending out into the Pacific beyond Singapore like a handful of broken beads. No European power yet controlled them, though more than one competed fiercely for their spice products.

"And here is a note about the secret strait that I will find—of which I know!"

He showed the king some writing on the globe about a *paso*, or strait, leading from the Atlantic to the ocean then called the Great South Sea—the Pacific. The exact location of the strait was not indicated.

Magellan planned to sail to the Moluccas through this strait, load a cargo of the valuable spices, and return. The only known sea route to the East was by the Cape of Good Hope, around Africa. But these waters and the lands in the Eastern Hemisphere had been allotted to Portugal by the Treaty of Tordesillas in 1494. A line had been established running north and south in the western Atlantic, passing through the bulge of Brazil.

Spain and Portugal, the two pioneers in early voyages of discovery, had agreed that the world *east* of this line would be exclusively Portugal's to explore and navigate. The regions *west* of the line would be Spain's.

Of course, there was a question in everyone's mind, since Spain and Portugal had sliced the world in two like an apple, as to how this line divided the Orient on the other side. Did it cut through China? through Japan? Were the Spice Islands on the Spanish or the Portuguese side? No one knew for certain because the problem of the earth's circumference was unsolved. You couldn't measure halfway around when you didn't know the distance all the way around.

Magellan was sure that the Spice Islands were in the Spanish zone. He had even said so when he was in the Portuguese service. Now he convinced Charles I and his advisers of this.

As for the business side of the project, that made Bishop Fonseca's eyes gleam and Cristóbal de Haro rub his hands. Spices were the uranium and oil of the sixteenth century, the source of fabulous fortunes. A bale of dried leaves selling for one ducat in the Indies brought one hundred ducats in London, a profit of 10,000 per cent! Cloves, ginger, and pepper were not only a luxury but a desperately sought necessity, taking the place of the modern refrigerator as preservers of meat through the long winters; at least they masked the odours of partially spoiled food and made a monotonous diet more palatable. Other spices were used as drugs.

Magellan was proposing to seek a route to the origin of this wealth through Spanish waters, a new inside track to prosperity.

But the scientific and heroic aspects of Magellan's scheme were even more impressive and perhaps carried greater weight with the idealistic young king. Magellan was proposing a voyage of thousands of miles, lasting two years, which would link the two halves of the known world— the Atlantic and the Indian Ocean areas. And if he returned by the familiar route around Africa, he would be circumnavigating the earth for the first time in history.

At the end of the interview the enthusiasm on Charles's face showed his approval. Bishop Fonseca and merchant de Haro secretly exchanged glances. For their own personal gain they were backing Magellan, but even they were surprised by the apparent swiftness of the king's decision. Indeed, in the months ahead Charles, who signed himself Yo, El Rey (I, the King), stood steadfastly behind Magellan as the obscure Portuguese prepared for the most difficult voyage yet attempted by man.

Magellan was destined to overcome tempests, mutiny, starvation, and despair, winning the accolade of a modern historian: "Undoubtedly the greatest of ancient and modern navigators." After his achievement no one could doubt that the earth is round. Men would know for the first time the width of the Pacific and how a calendar day is lost in the westward circumnavigation. An estimate of the circumference of the earth made by Amerigo Vespucci in the early 1500's would be proved accurate.

The strait discovered at the tip of South America would be known as the Strait of Magellan; two southern star clusters would be listed as Magellanic; and the South Sea would henceforth bear the name Magellan gave it—the Pacific—when he first entered its vast expanse of blue and gold.

Who was this unheralded veteran who now picked up his painted globe and, accompanied by his eccentric astronomer partner and his faithful Malayan slave, limped from the throne room?

Who was Ferdinand Magellan?

In the first place, he was not known as Magellan until near the end of his life, but as Magalhães, which was the Portuguese form of his name. Fernão de Magalhães—whom we will call by the better-known "Magellan," the English form derived from the Spanish "Magallanes"—was born about 1480 in north Portugal, in the province of Entre-Douro-e-Minho.

The first Magellan to enter Portugal had come from France in the eleventh century. He had ridden, like the hero Roland, over the mountain passes to fight the Moors, the Mohammedan inhabitants of the Spanish peninsula who had held the land for several centuries. Now the Moors were being driven out by the Christian kings of northern and central Spain, aided by crusading knights from all over Europe. Ferdinand's ancestor fought under Count Henry of Burgundy, founder of the kingdom of Portugal, and was rewarded with a modest estate at a place called Ponte da Barca.

Here Ferdinand, his older brother, Diogo, and his sister, Isabel, grew up. They played hide-and-seek in the Magellan Tower, a tumble-down fortress once used against the Moors but now converted to serve as the family residence. They climbed up into the hills surrounding their fertile farm to collect chestnuts or hunt rabbits.

Not long after his twelfth birthday Ferdinand found himself a page at the court of Queen Leonora in Lisbon. His father was a *fidalgo* (the fourth of five grades of nobility), and it was the custom for the lesser Portuguese nobles to seek advantages for their sons by sending them to court as pages. Ferdinand's brother, Diogo, was already there. Diogo, Ferdinand, and their lively cousin Francisco Serrano became inseparable companions.

They wore the queen's colours, carried messages for the officials, and studied music, dancing, hunting, and horsemanship together. But what Ferdinand especially liked was maritime science—map-making and a simple astronomy which showed him how to take the altitude of the sun or the north star and plot a ship's position.

In 1493 a storm-battered ship sailed up the Tagus River to the harbour of Lisbon and set them all wild with excitement. The ship was the *Niña*, back from the discovery of America, bearing Christopher Columbus, his crew, and some long-haired, brown-skinned captives.

Of course for days Lisbon talked of nothing but Columbus's voyage. The Portuguese were envious because for eighty years their expeditions had been inching down the coast of Africa, seeking a sea route to the riches of the East.

But Columbus had reached the East first. Perhaps he had even sailed into their area, allotted them by Pope Alexander VI. Perhaps Portugal would have war with Spain!

Instead of war, however, shrewd King John of Portugal obtained a new agreement with Spain, the Treaty of Tordesillas, which moved the line of demarcation many miles west into the Atlantic. It turned out that even part of Brazil lay east of this line, in the Portuguese zone. And as the years passed, men suspected that Columbus had not reached Asia, after all, but some unheard-of new land on the way.

It was truly an age of discovery that young Ferdinand Magellan found himself living in, the second great age of discovery in history. The first had come in the fourth century B.C. with the conquests of Alexander the Great, opening up the Indian Ocean to the West. After Alexander, Greek thinkers had fitted together a picture of the world that was accurate—as far as it went.

Aristotle, Alexander's tutor, demonstrated by two arguments that the earth is not flat but a sphere. First, as you travel north or south familiar stars disappear and new ones take their places; this could not happen if the earth was flat. Second, during an eclipse of the moon, in which the earth passes between the sun and the moon, the earth always casts a curved shadow on the moon; if the earth was not spherical, its shadow would not *always* be curved.

A century later Eratosthenes, the founder of mathematical geography, figured out from the angle of the sun's rays the circumference of the earth: 25,000 miles. (Unfortunately his findings were afterward discarded for a smaller, wrong figure.)

Still later, around 150 A.D., another geographer and astronomer named Ptolemy gathered in two volumes (the *Almagest*, and the *Geographia*) most of the Greek knowledge of the universe. His maps showed the continents of Europe, Asia, and Africa; but he erred in making the Indian Ocean a closed sea by connecting the bottom of Africa with the bottom of eastern Asia. He sketched the stars and planets as we know them, but he placed the earth instead of the sun at the centre of the system.

In the Middle Ages certain scholars revived the old idea that the earth is flat; if you sailed too far, they believed, you might fall off. Equally misleading was the theory that the fierce, direct rays of the sun would not permit life to exist at the equator, and that white men sailing into the Torrid Zone would turn black. But geographers who believed the earth was a sphere eventually triumphed. Experienced captains also knew that the earth is round, because they had seen a ship sink below the horizon in the distance or an island apparently rise out of the horizon when approached.

Still, those were brave mariners from Magellan's Portugal who, in the fifteenth century, sailed south into the unknown. They rediscovered or explored the Azores, Madeiras, and Canaries—the island groups out in the Atlantic; they reached one cape after another until they cleared Cape Verde, Africa's westernmost point, and

went on to the rich Gold Coast. At last, in 1487, Bartholomew Diaz rounded the Cape of Good Hope (which
he called the Cape of Storms), disproving Ptolemy's belief
that the Indian Ocean was enclosed by land. The Portuguese had circled Africa and now stood on the threshold
of the East.

How did these early explorers find their way in the
immense "Ocean Sea" without radio or modern instruments of navigation?

First of all, ever since Ptolemy's *Geographia* they had
had a "street plan" of the world. Invisible avenues and
streets called "longitudes" and "latitudes" had been traced
over the globe. If a navigator could locate himself with
reference to these, he knew where he was.

The "parallels" of latitude—which were all that sixteenth
century navigators could really determine—run, like cross
streets, horizontally around the world. So a sailor voyaging
"up" or "down"—say, from the Congo "up" to Great
Britain—could figure how many lines, or degrees, of latitude he had crossed. The equator, the parallel around the
middle of the earth, is 0° latitude. The sailor would measure the lines, or degrees, he had crossed north or south of
the equator. Great Britain begins at about 50° north latitude, that is, 50° north of the equator. The North Pole,
which is at a right angle to any spot on the equator, would
be 90° north latitude, the South Pole 90° south latitude.

To make use of this "street plan" the sixteenth-century
mariner relied on a few simple instruments: the compass,
to tell him what direction he was sailing in; and the
astrolabe or the cross-staff to determine his latitude, his
distance (in degrees) north or south of the equator.

If a sailor could measure the height of the sun at noon,
and if he had a table giving some technical data about the

position of the sun in relation to the celestial equator, he could compute his latitude.

Such tables of the declination of the sun were available in the sixteenth century. And with the astrolabe or the cross-staff the mariner could take a sight on the sun or, better, the north star, whose altitude (in degrees) *is* the exact latitude of the observer. The astrolabe was a disk with a pointer on it, like a clock with only one hand. The cross-staff was two pieces of wood fitted together like the letter T. Both were graduated in degrees.

But what about longitude? The avenues, or meridians, of longitude run from the North Pole at the top of the world to the South Pole at the bottom. They are like the lines running from top to bottom of a peeled orange, dividing it into sections. In Magellan's time the sailor going *around* the world, say from Africa to South America, could try to figure how many lines, or degrees, of longitude he had crossed. He could call one line, say the line through the Canary Islands just off the African coast, 0° and figure his longitude "west" or "east" of that line. Going all the way around the world would mean crossing 360 meridians, since the circumference of a circle is 360°.

Unfortunately, in practice a ship's exact east-west position at sea was not to be known until two hundred years later, when the chronometer was invented. Navigators in Magellan's day merely guessed at their longitude from their direction and their rate of speed.

The rate of speed was determined by tossing an object over the prow of the ship and timing its drift to the stern with a sandglass. Sometimes the captain simply spat and timed *that*. Five miles an hour, a brisk walking pace, was considered a fair speed.

With these crude instruments, and in ships not much

more than ninety feet from stem to stern, men were preparing to sail halfway around the earth. Young Ferdinand Magellan could hardly wait to go.

In 1496 Magellan and his friends were raised to the rank of squire and made clerks in the Marine Department established by the new King Manuel. And in 1497 the Portuguese under Vasco da Gama not only rounded the Cape of Good Hope again but reached India. Although the Arabs, who monopolized the oriental trade, were hostile, the Portuguese immediately took part in the rich spice traffic. Wealth began to pour into impoverished Portugal, and a "gold rush" to the Indies started.

In the next twenty-five years nearly one fifth of the males of little Portugal, whose total population was about a million, would be drained off overseas. Practically all the younger men left to seek their fortunes. Many died, but some returned as "pepperbags"—rich merchants whose wealth was founded on spices.

Poor Magellan, though, had to labour on for several years as a clerk, outfitting fleets in which others with more influence at court sailed first. He trudged down the hills of Lisbon to nautical shops for maps, compasses, astrolabes, and hourglasses, or checked with ship chandlers along the waterfront. While there he gazed longingly at the high-castled caravels and *naos* (merchant ships) anchored in the Tagus River.

At last Ferdinand Magellan, his brother, and Francisco Serrano were appointed supernumeraries in the fleet of Viceroy Francisco de Almeida, an able and courageous naval commander. A supernumerary was not a member of the crew but a volunteer of gentle birth who would be called upon for fighting. Since Almeida's orders were to set up bases along the east coast of Africa and the west coast of India, in hostile territory, Magellan's services would certainly be needed.

Like our American pioneers, the daring Almeida was going to build forts to control a region in which his fighting men would be outnumbered. His aim was to wrest the oriental trade from the Arabs and Egyptians (backed by Venice) and establish a Portuguese monopoly. He spearheaded the first European colonialism in Asia and Africa.

Magellan was twenty-five years old, a short, firm-jawed young man, when in March, 1505, he first felt the long swell of the Atlantic beneath his feet. He stood beside his sea chest and blanket roll, in the tiny space allotted him in the waist of the caravel, and glanced from the great square sails on which the red crusaders' cross of the Knights of Christ was painted, to the dark coast of Africa they were skirting. He was ambitious and devout. He dreamed of fame and fortune, then each day at dusk joined wholeheartedly in the chanting of the Latin hymn to the Blessed Virgin Mary, the *Salve Regina*, led by the gallant viceroy himself.

Among Magellan's thoughts, even this early, may have been speculations about a westward route to India. Throughout his life he showed interest in "westist" theories. As a worker in the Marine Department he was familiar with the discovery of Brazil by the Portuguese Cabral in 1500 and the exploration of its coast. And he never forgot the arrival of Columbus in Lisbon.

Through stinging hail and snow, buffeted by continual gales, Almeida's fleet doubled the Cape of Good Hope. In July, 1505, they entered the harbour of Kilwa, Tanzania, then the most important city of East Africa. Here Magellan spent the next two years. He was stationed in the

Portuguese garrison and served on a light vessel which patrolled the coast, chasing Arab smugglers.

In October, 1507, Magellan arrived, under orders, in India. His ship docked at Cochin, the Portuguese colonial capital near the tip of India on its western side. He was immediately caught up in the excitement of the Portuguese drive to conquer the East.

First he was assigned to a caravel and learned how these ships were manoeuvered. In battle their captains kept just beyond bowshot of the clumsy Arab dhows and bombarded them. The Portuguese aimed especially for the rudders and masts of the enemy. Since the dhows were not strong enough to carry cannon, the Arabs were helpless, in spite of their superior numbers, unless they could close with the Portuguese ships and board them. But the caravels kept their distance until their broadsides had disabled the Arabs. These tactics eventually won important posts in the East for Portugal.

The caravels under their clouds of canvas fanned out over the Indian Ocean like covered wagons crossing the plains. One mission took Magellan to the Island of Ceylon. Then the caravels gathered for the climactic battle. On December 12, 1508, the war fleet of Almeida, nineteen vessels bearing thirteen hundred Portuguese and four hundred Indians, set sail from Cananore, near Cochin, their prows pointed north-west towards the upper Arabian Sea.

On February 2, 1509, off the city of Diu in the north-west corner of India, they sighted the enemy—one hundred Egyptian and Indian ships flying the banners of the Sultan of Egypt. Grimly Almeida advanced toward the foe.

The Portuguese followed their usual tactics, taking the position from which the wind was blowing. Cannon were wheeled forward, and the thunder of Almeida's broadside echoed across the water. The dhows could not head into the wind to grapple with the Portuguese. Masts toppled, rudders were ripped into the sea. Then, at a sharp command, the caravels came about and bore down upon the confused mass of the Eyptian-Indian fleet.

Magellan's ship closed with the flagship of the Turkish admiral, Mir Hocem. A wave of fighting men, Magellan among them, poured over the bulwarks and smashed into the mail-clad Mamelukes, the admiral's personal bodyguard. Five hours later the standard of Portugal was raised on the masthead of the bloodstained Egyptian flagship. But Magellan's captain was dead, and Magellan himself lay severely wounded in the jumble of bodies.

The Battle of Diu was over, one of the decisive battles in world history. Portuguese dominance in the Indian Ocean was assured. Henceforth most of Europe's imports from the Orient would be carried around Africa in Portuguese vessels rather than delivered by Arabs through Egypt to Venice.

Magellan had scarcely recovered from his wounds before he was sent on another expedition, under Captain Sequeira. The object of Sequeira's armada was to strengthen Portuguese control of the East by pushing on to Malacca, in the Malay Peninsula. The Portuguese wished to conquer Malacca and eventually make it the eastern anchor of their empire. Malacca would play the role of modern Singapore (located nearby) as the great market centre of the East Indies.

In September, 1509, Magellan stared from the deck of his cumbrous transport, loaded with cavalry horses, at this picturesque city. Malacca spread endlessly along the shore, with palm groves, minarets, gardens, and mansions looming behind. Chinese, Malay, and Arab ships covered the water;

A drawing of
Lisbon
Harbour in the
early 16th
century

(From de Bry's
Americae III,
1592)

on the quay slaves, porcelain, spices, sandalwood, and gems were bargained for in a babel of languages. Only the harbour front was lined with high brown ramparts bearing brass cannon pointing at the Portuguese ships.

Magellan did not know that Sultan Mohammed, having learned of the Portuguese advance into the Indian Ocean, was plotting to capture the intruders. Mohammed received the Portuguese blandly, offering spices and jewels at remarkably favourable prices. Malay dignitaries in stately galleys, rowed to the rhythm of drums and cymbals, visited the Portuguese flagship and played chess with Sequeira.

At the last moment Francisco Serrano learned of the plot from a native woman. He rushed to the wharf to warn the Portuguese seamen bartering there and tried frantically to signal the fleet. Magellan, perched in the maintop of his ship, saw sampans suspiciously crowded with muscular "merchants" bearing down on the vessels. He glimpsed Serrano waving like a wild man from the dock. Not delaying a second, Magellan raced down the ropes, rowed to the flagship, and spoke to Sequeira, bent over his chessmen, in Portuguese.

The alert captain-general promptly overturned the chessboard in the Malays' faces just as one of them was drawing his dagger. The Malays were driven from the deck. Magellan jumped into a skiff, rowed to the wharf, and, after a bitter struggle, rescued Serrano and a few others. The fleet hoisted sail and escaped, but thirty Portuguese were killed and thirty captured. One day the Portuguese would come back in great force for vengeance.

On his return voyage to India Magellan's transport was attacked by Chinese pirates. Magellan led a counterattack and almost single-handed captured the pirate junk. For his bravery he was promoted to the rank of captain and given command of a caravel.

Officials in the Portuguese empire were being changed, however, and these changes affected Magellan's prospects. Under King Manuel the Fortunate, admirals were unfortunate. King Manuel was a gangling, earnest man who excelled in sports and was a keen judge of ability. His programme of building new cathedrals, monasteries, and hospitals gave employment to the poor and adorned his kingdom. He pushed the expansion of Portugal overseas and chose the right men for the task. But as soon as a loyal commander, like Almeida, achieved great success, the envious king would dismiss him in favour of another.

Thus he had treated Vasco da Gama, first to reach India around the Cape of Good Hope, and thus he treated Almeida, who was now dispatched, broken-hearted, to Portugal while his replacement, Albuquerque, took command.

Ruddy, bearded Alonso de Albuquerque, a strong-minded leader who did not like opposition, possessed all of Almeida's courage plus unusual administrative ability. He was to consolidate the empire won by Almeida's naval victories, basing it firmly on four great land fortresses ringing the Indian Ocean—Malacca, Goa, and Ormuz, all of which he captured, and Aden, which submitted shortly after his death. He was far-seeing and just, but at the same time headstrong.

Almeida's veterans were slighted by the new regime. So Magellan stacked his precious sacks of pepper, his shares of the various prizes, his "Malabar money," on a caravel and sailed for home. In Portugal he would be modestly wealthy, even if not a millionaire "pepperbag." He could settle down as a country gentleman and spend the rest of his life in leisure.

In the middle of the Indian Ocean, however, Magellan had bad luck. His ship crashed on the Shoals of Padua, a hundred miles from Cananore. Although captain, crew, and passenger *fidalgos* escaped in a longboat to a nearby atoll, Magellan was a ruined man, his pepper spoiled by the waves.

A sister ship was grounded a short distance away, and its survivors rowed to the same atoll. Then a pitched battle almost broke out, for the senior captain ruled that since there was not room for everyone in the two longboats, only the noble *fidalgos* might depart. They would row to Cochin and send a rescue ship for the others.

The common seamen protested violently and seized the water supply. With his usual presence of mind and unselfishness, Magellan made peace by offering, though himself a *fidalgo*, to stay with the crews. Just before the *fidalgos* left, though, Magellan happened to be in one of the longboats talking to them, and a suspicious seaman shouted, "*Senhor*, did you not promise to stay with us?"

"Yes, I did," replied Magellan, jumping out of the boat to splash ashore. "And here I am!"

On his return to India three weeks later, Magellan tried to recoup his fortune but failed. Worse, his old habit of speaking his mind brought about his final downfall. When Albuquerque asked his caravel captains whether he should seize some private ships to aid in a battle, Magellan replied that taking the ships would be both unnecessary and unjust. Albuquerque was furious—and commandeered the ships anyhow.

Later Magellan fought at the capture of Malacca (1511), and still later (1512) took his caravel on a mysterious

cruise, possibly all the way to the Philippines. He was seeking information about the coveted Spice Islands. Unfortunately when he got back he expressed the conviction that
the Spice Islands did not lie in the longitudes assigned to
Portugal but in those of her arch-rival, Spain!

Albuquerque and King Manuel considered this honest
opinion almost traitorous. Magellan was quietly relieved
of his command and ordered back to Portugal. His eight
years of service in the Indies were over, and he had only
about a thousand pounds to show for it—less than he could
have earned as a clerk, safe in Lisbon.

But he had displayed matchless courage and coolness
under fire. He had come to know the East as few men
then knew it. And he had become one of the world's most
skilful navigators.

Upon his return in 1513 Magellan found Lisbon much
changed. The once sleepy harbour was a wilderness of
masts and sails; mansions and towered churches lined both
sides of the Tagus River. When Magellan entered the
splendid India House, no one gave him a second look.

The bureaucrats were too busy getting rich themselves
to waste time on an impoverished veteran, even though
their wealth had been won with his blood.

A disdainful clerk informed Magellan that he would
probably be promoted from squire to gentleman-in-waiting—he, a hero of the Orient, one of the victors with Almeida and Albuquerque! Magellan was proud of his record.
He promptly applied for the higher rank of *cavaleiro
fidalgo*, cavalier of the household—the least he deserved.

More important, he hoped to regain King Manuel's
favour so that he could captain a caravel on a voyage back
to the Moluccas. His cousin Francisco Serrano had re-

cently become assistant to the king and a power behind the throne on Ternate, one of the Spice Islands. Serrano wrote to Magellan, begging him to bring Portuguese reinforcements and offering a rich cargo of spices in return. Perhaps Magellan already had in mind a westward passage to India.

To attract King Manuel's attention, Magellan volunteered for a Portuguese military expedition being sent against rebels in Morocco. At that time the Portuguese were conquering ports and small territories on the Atlantic seaboard of North Africa. In the fighting around the key city of Azamor, March, 1514, Magellan was wounded in the knee and lamed for life.

To reward Magellan for his valuable services on the staff, the commander of the army made him provost marshal and placed all the prisoners and captured booty in his care. Actually the commander was giving Magellan a chance to become rich, because it was customary for the provost marshal to "liberate" many of these captured treasures for himself. But Magellan was a stubbornly honest man. He took nothing—and then found himself accused of graft and of selling captured horses to the enemy by some jealous officers who wanted his position.

Magellan scornfully ignored these charges and returned to Portugal. He finally secured his royal audience. But King Manuel brushed aside his request for a caravel. Staring at Magellan with his large eyes and clenching his suspicious mouth, he ordered him back to Morocco to clear himself.

Doggedly Magellan retraced his steps and won a verdict of "not proved." When Magellan was once more in Portugal, King Manuel refused to see him a second time.

Magellan was miserable. Two years had dragged by, he had been given neither promotion nor employment, and his meagre savings were tied up in a lawsuit. Tormented by his longing to return to the East, he took a rash step. By tipping an attendant, he had his name added to the list of commoners who were to be received publicly by the king.

No one of noble birth ever appeared among these humble suitors. When "Magellan!" was called, there was a stir of astonishment among the courtiers.

Ferdinand Magellan limped through the beribboned, perfumed aristocrats and knelt at the steps of the dais, a small figure before his tall, displeased king. In a stumbling voice he asked first for his promotion, then for command of a caravel to sail to the Moluccas.

"No," said King Manuel abruptly to both pleas.

Manuel disliked the embarrassing position Magellan had placed him in—and he disliked Magellan.

Magellan was crimson. He knew he should kiss the royal hand and depart, but he seemed rooted to the dais. A resentment he could not suppress welled up.

"Do I have Your Majesty's permission, then," he heard himself asking in a strained, defiant tone, "to serve some other lord?"

"I do not care what you do or where you go," said King Manuel and turned his back on his humiliated subject.

Somehow Magellan made his way out of the palace, out of Lisbon. He fled up the coast to Oporto, where he lived in complete obscurity, speaking to no one except a few other veterans.

It was in this period of suffering (1516–17) that he met the fiery astronomer Ruy Faleiro. Together they forged the idea that would later result in Magellan's immortal accomplishment, the voyage west around the world. Faleiro, too, was unemployed. Although the best scholar in his field, he had been passed over for a court favourite when he applied for the position of Royal Astronomer, partly because of his jealous, unstable nature.

The two outcasts discussed their theories night after night in the smoky taverns of Oporto. Faleiro explained his new method of determining longitude. Old pilot friends of Magellan's dropped by to contribute their knowledge. One of them even arranged for Magellan to be admitted to the royal chartroom in Lisbon to examine the maps and globes there. And so Magellan became obsessed with the idea of reaching the Spice Islands by sailing west—if not in the service of Portugal, then for some other nation.

A Portuguese navigator would think of just one other nation, the one which, in Magellan's opinion, already had a just claim to the Moluccas—Spain. Both da Gama and Almeida at different times had planned to enter the Spanish service because of King Manuel's ingratitude.

Then came a summons from fate. In India Magellan had become friendly with an influential businessman, Duarte Barbosa. Duarte now visited his uncle Diogo Barbosa, who had given up his Portuguese citizenship and become governor of the Castle of Seville. Duarte learned that his uncle and other leading Spaniards were going to send an expedition to the East by the western route.

"Ferdinand Magellan of Portugal is an excellent navigator, is unemployed, and is interested in the westward voyage," Duarte told the Spaniards.

Whereupon, in the summer of 1517, the command of this Spanish expedition to the Moluccas was offered to Magellan. Details would be worked out upon his arrival in Spain, and Charles I's consent would have to be gained.

Magellan was approaching forty. He would carry to his grave the scars received fighting for Portugal. His life seemed to have been only a succession of failures. When the Spaniards agreed to employ Faleiro also, Magellan made his decision.

He denaturalized himself, that is, renounced his Portuguese citizenship; then he boarded a ship in the harbour of Oporto and left for a new country and a new career.

Five battered merchánt *naos* lay tilted on the ways of a small shipyard at the Dock of the Mules in Seville. Wooden mallets rang as bad planks were replaced and gun decks strengthened. Caulkers drove oakum into the seams.

This was Magellan's fleet. And Captain-General Magellan was everywhere, cheerfully directing repairs, while the Portuguese consul, one Alvarez, looked on and sniffed.

"Their ribs are as soft as butter," Alvarez wrote to King Manuel. "I would be sorry to sail even for the Canaries in them."

Alvarez, a persistent, arrogant man, had instructions to sabotage the expedition in any way possible. King Manuel would give no employment to Magellan himself but was enraged when Charles I did. Besides, Manuel claimed the disputed Spice Islands for Portugal!

Magellan remained buoyant. He had recently married the charming Lady Beatriz, daughter of Governor Diogo Barbosa. In July, 1518, Charles made him a Knight Commander of the Order of Santiago, and in September Beatriz presented him with a son and heir, Rodrigo.

There were difficulties, however, caused by people who were plotting Magellan's ruin. In October, 1518, Consul Alvarez instigated a serious riot at the wharves. When Magellan launched his flagship, the *Trinidad*, without flying the royal standard (it was at the flagmaker's being repainted), Alvarez's agents inflamed the dock idlers.

"See! He leaves off our flag—he insults our country!"

B

they muttered. "This Magellan is a Portuguese spy! He is going to steal the fleet for Portugal!"

Worse, Magellan's captain's standards, which *were* displayed, bore the arms of the king of Portugal as part of the Magellan family coat of arms. Soon stones were flying through the air. Magellan's workers were routed, and the captain-general himself was wounded in the hand. When King Charles heard about this, he punished the idlers severely.

Then Bishop Fonseca began to scheme to put his own followers in important positions. He had backed Magellan at first and still wanted the expedition to succeed, but he hoped to seize the profits for himself. He thought the terms granted to Magellan by King Charles were too generous. His master plan was to have Magellan replaced at sea by his nephew, Juan Cartagena.

He had three of his henchmen, including Cartagena, chosen as ship captains and also secured the appointment of Estevan Gomes as chief pilot. Although Gomes was a distant relative of Magellan's, he was very jealous of him because Gomes had earlier been considered for Magellan's post—and rejected. Magellan, only half aware of these resentments, signed on as many experienced Portuguese as he could. His cousin Juan Serrano, brother of Francisco Serrano who awaited them in the distant Moluccas, was Magellan's one faithful ship captain.

Because of the low pay it was difficult to find seamen for the voyage. Recruiting officers unfurled banners of the king in the squares and on the piers of Seville. This was followed by a ruffle of drums.

"Join the Armada and see the wonders of an unknown world!" the heralds cried. "Rubies and pearls for the asking!"

The lounging sailors only grimaced. They translated the

glowing words into "back-breaking labour, sickness, and danger." Eventually Magellan pieced out his crew with a mixture of Spaniards, Portuguese, Italians, Basques, Frenchmen, Germans, Moors, and others, including one Englishman—Master Andrew of Bristol, master gunner of the fleet.

Ruy Faleiro, Magellan's touchy astronomer partner, became so unreasonable that he had to be left behind. A rumour spread that he had cast his horoscope and learned that he would die if he sailed with the expedition. A young Venetian who arrived one day with credentials from Charles I proved a welcome addition. This was Antonio Pigafetta. He signed on as a supernumerary and became Magellan's great admirer and the historian of the voyage.

The cargo was carefully chosen for the profitable trade which Magellan's backers anticipated. Cristóbal de Haro, who was putting up much of the money, selected quicksilver, fishhooks, knives, basins, bracelets, and copper bars (for the coinage mints of the East). In addition there was coloured cotton cloth, brocade, velvet, lace, hand mirrors, ornamental combs, and thousands of tinkling little bells—all designed to make the eyes of Eastern ladies sparkle. In return Magellan would load his ships with precious spices. Magellan tried to check every item but did not know that Consul Alvarez was bribing officials to withhold supplies.

In August, 1519, the entire company of the fleet with their families attended a solemn High Mass in the Church of Santa Maria de la Victoria near the dockyard. Magellan received the royal silken standard of the king. Then the four ship captains knelt before him at the altar and swore in firm, loud voices to obey him. (Three of them, however, had just agreed to murder Magellan at the first opportunity!)

On August 10, a Monday, the fleet sailed from Seville.

A broadside echoed over the red tile roofs. A leisurely trip of seventy-five miles down the Guadalquivir River brought them to the ocean port of San Lúcar.

Here they delayed a month while Magellan and de Haro worked at correcting shortages which they had discovered. Alvarez had spent his bribe money well. Even then, the deficiencies in ship's biscuit, salt beef, salt pork, peas, honey, olives, and other foods were not fully realized.

At last, on September 20, 1519, the *Trinidad*, *San Antonio*, *Concepción*, *Victoria*, and *Santiago* weighed anchor—setting out on a longer, more perilous voyage than even Columbus had endured. Magellan had put in writing for his friend El Rey his evidence that the Spice Islands really did belong to Charles. He had made his will, providing for his son Rodrigo and for the Lady Beatriz, who was soon to give birth to their second child.

A favouring wind filled the sails. Crews waved from the crowded decks to wives and sweethearts. The line of ships stood out of the harbour, Magellan's *Trinidad* in the lead.

Over two hundred men (estimates range from 241 to 280) headed into the Atlantic that day. Three years later eighteen half-starved survivors would return in the *Victoria*.

Ferdinand Magellan would not be among them.

But the world would never be the same again. Its widest ocean would have been spanned, its farthest people greeted, its measure taken. The great navigator's final legacy was to be not only riches for Spain but knowledge for all mankind.

CHAPTER ONE

A NEW ROUTE TO THE EAST

March 22, 1518 — August 10, 1519

Look where the oceans of the Orient lie,
With their infinity of islands sown,
Tidore and Ternate, whence on high
From his hot crest the waves of fire are thrown.
There trees of burning cloves you may descry . . .
And there the golden birds that ne'er descend
To earth, hence never seen till their lives end.

—*The Lusiads*, CAMOËNS

DIVIDING THE WORLD

At the time of Magellan's voyage large areas of the earth were still unknown to men in Europe. Maximilian of Transylvania, in the following pages, tells some of the things men did not know—for example, whether the American coastline was solid and unbroken, or whether a ship could find an opening between "Cod-fish Land" (Newfoundland), "Florida," and "Terra Firma" (South America), and sail to the East.

The selection from Maximilian also shows the attempts to regulate sixteenth-century exploration by treaties. Immediately after Columbus's discovery of America, Ferdinand and Isabella urged Pope Alexander VI, a fellow Spaniard, to declare the new lands theirs by a papal bull, which the pope did in 1493.

It is often said that the pope divided the world between Spain and Portugal. Actually he only intended to help Spain; Portugal is not mentioned in the bull. The pope granted Spain all new lands discovered one thousand miles or more west of the Cape Verde Islands in the Atlantic.

By the Treaty of Tordesillas (1494) the politicians of the two countries revised the papal bull and declared that everything found fifteen hundred miles or more west of the Cape Verde Islands belonged to Spain; everything east of this "line of demarcation," to Portugal. The line of demarcation was never exactly drawn, partly because it was defined in "leagues" distant from the Cape Verde Islands and there was no agreement about how long a league was. In practice the line coincided with present-day 46° 30′ west longitude, cutting through Brazil.

The statesmen's intention was to divide up "spheres of influence" in the Atlantic, but by the time Magellan sailed their thinking had become global. Spain now claimed everything west of the line of demarcation to the other side of the earth, Portugal everything to the east. Maximilian tells us how sure Magellan was that the Moluccas were in the Spanish half of the globe (in fact, they were not), and how he convinced King Charles of this and received his commission.

The following passage is taken from Maximilian's *De Moluccis Insulis* (*Concerning the Spice Islands*, 1523), the first published account of Magellan's voyage. Maximilian was a secretary at the court of King Charles.

When, nearly thirty years ago [1493], the Spaniards in the west, and the Portuguese in the east, began to search for new and unknown lands, their two kings, lest one should be a hindrance to the other, divided the whole globe between them by the authority, most likely, of Pope Alexander [Borgia] the Sixth, in this manner: that a straight line should be drawn 360 . . . leagues west of the islands of the Hesperides, which are now called the islands of Cape Verde; toward the north, and another toward the south Pole, till they should meet again, and so divide the world into two equal parts. And whatever strange land should be discovered eastward of this line should be ceded to the Portuguese, and whatever west of it to the Spaniards.

In this manner it happened that the Spaniards always sailed southwest, and there they discovered a very large continent and very great and innumerable islands, rich in gold and pearls and in other wealth, and now, quite lately, have they discovered the vast . . . city, Tenochtitlán [Mexico City], situated in a lake, like Venice. . . .

But the Portuguese, passing southward by the shores of the Hesperides . . . and crossing the equinoctial line [the equator] and the Tropic of Capricorn, sailed eastward, and discovered many great and unknown islands. . . . Thence they sailed past the Arabian and Persian Gulfs to the shores of India, within the Ganges, where there is now the mighty emporium and kingdom of Calicut. Thence they sailed to Taprobanes, which they now call Sumatra. . . .

Going thence, they arrived at the Golden Chersonesus [the Malay Peninsula], where now is situated that most famous city of Malacca, the greatest emporium of the East. After this they entered the Great Gulf [the South China Sea], which reaches as far as . . . China. . . .

And though there was a certain rumour afloat that the Portuguese had progressed so far to the East as to cross their own limits and enter the territory of the Spaniards, and that Malacca and the Great Bay were within our limits, still all these things were said rather than believed, until four years ago Ferdinand Magellan, a distinguished Portuguese, who, for many years had explored the coasts of the whole of the East as Admiral, took a great hatred to his king, whom he complained of as being most ungrateful to him, and came to Caesar [Charles I of Spain].

Cristóbal de Haro, too, my own father-in-law's brother, who had traded for many years in the East by means of his agents, he himself staying in . . . Lisbon, and who had lastly traded with the Chinese, so that he has great practice in such things, having also been unjustly treated by the King of Portugal, came also home to Spain.

And they both showed Caesar [Charles] that though it was not yet quite sure whether Malacca was within the confines of the Spaniards or the Portuguese, because, as yet, nothing of the longitude had been clearly proved, yet that it was quite plain that the Great Gulf and the people of China lay within the Spanish boundary. This, too, was held to be most certain, that the islands which they call the Moluccas, in which all the spices are produced, and are thence exported to Malacca, lay within the Spanish western division, and that it was possible to sail there; and that spices could be brought thence to Spain more easily, and at less expense and cheaper, as they came direct from their native place.

Their course would be this, to sail westward, coasting the southern hemisphere till they came to the East. The thing seemed almost impossible and useless, not because it was thought a difficult thing to go from the west right to the east under the hemisphere, but because it was uncertain whether ingenious nature, which has done nothing without the greatest foresight, had not so dissevered the east from the west, partly by sea and partly by land, as to make it impossible to arrive there by either land or sea travelling.

For it had not then been discovered whether that

great region which is called Terra Firma [South America] did [wholly] separate the western sea from the eastern; it was clear enough that that continent, in its southern part, trended southward and afterward westward. It was clear, also, that two regions had been discovered in the north, one of which they called Regio Bacalearum (Cod-fish Land) [Newfoundland], from a new kind of fish; and the other Terra Florida.

And if these two were united to that Terra Firma, it was impossible to get to the east [the Orient] by going from the west, as nothing had ever been discovered of any channel through this land, though it had been sought for most diligently and with great labour. And they considered it a very doubtful and most dangerous enterprise to go through the limits of the Portuguese [around Africa], and so to the east.

For which reason it seemed to Caesar [Charles] and to his counsellors that these men were promising a thing from which much was to be hoped, but still of great difficulty. When they were both brought to an audience on a certain day, Magellan offered to go himself, but Cristóbal de Haro offered to fit out a fleet at his own expense and that of his friends, but only if it were allowed to sail under the authority and protection of Caesar [Charles]. Whilst they both persisted rather obstinately in their offers, Caesar [Charles] himself equipped a fleet of five ships, and appointed Magellan its admiral.

Their orders were, to sail southward along the coast

of Terra Firma till they found either its termination or some channel through which they might reach the spice-bearing Moluccas.

A GLOBE AND A PLAN

Bartolomé de Las Casas, the good bishop and "Apostle of the Indies," was present at the interview between Magellan and Charles I at the Spanish court in Valladolid. He gives his impressions of this meeting in the account that follows.

The "well-painted globe" which Magellan displayed may have been one copied from the work of the famous geographer Martin Behaim. If it was a Behaim globe, Magellan probably thought that South America was a southeastern peninsula of Asia because Behaim's globe showed a world with only three continents (Europe, Asia, and Africa), with only one ocean instead of two lying between Europe and Asia. Behaim's globe gave Asia a southeastern peninsula whose eastern coast sufficiently resembled the east coast of South America to make Magellan think that South America was a part of Asia. Taking South America for this peninsula, Magellan would expect to find a strait in its southern parts and to sail through the strait to Ptolemy's "Great Gulf," an Asian bay in which the Moluccas would be located. As late as 1540—long after Magellan's voyage—some geographers still considered the newly discovered Americas to be a part of Asia.

For the geographers of Magellan's day, everything between the fraction of South America that had been explored and Asia was a blur, a vaguely known or guessed-at region of ocean and islands. The ocean, which turned out to be enormously wider than anyone imagined, was variously called the South Sea, the Great Gulf, the Eastern Ocean, and so forth. If Magellan interpreted South America as the Behaim peninsula, his task was to find the hoped-for strait at its tip and sail through to the Moluccas. On the voyage he assured his men that after they passed through the strait they would have an easy sail of only a few weeks to the Spice Islands.

On the other hand, a later globe, made by Schöner in 1515, depicted the New World and seemed almost to anticipate Magellan by showing a strait between "America" (South America) and "Brasilie regio" (the Antarctic continent), not far from where Magellan actually found his strait. Schöner's globe was based on a report of an earlier, mysterious Portuguese voyage to South America backed by Cristóbal de Haro, who was now backing Magellan. If Magellan had inside information about this voyage from de Haro, he may have relied chiefly on this information rather than the outdated Behaim globe in his search for the strait.

Or he may have been most strongly influenced by the Spanish expedition of Juan de Solis to the La Plata River, in Argentina, in 1516. For a while this broad estuary was thought to be the passage to the South Sea. When Magellan reached it on his voyage, he, like de Solis, was at first confident that he had found the strait.

All such maps, reports of voyages, etc., were top secret in the sixteenth century; in 1504 King Manuel decreed the death penalty for anyone publishing unauthorized information about Portuguese discoveries. Because of this secrecy the details of Magellan's plan are obscure.

The following passage is taken from Las Casas' *Historia de las Indias*, written in the sixteenth century but not published until 1875–76.

Magellan had a well-painted globe on which the whole world was depicted, and on it he indicated the

Globe made by Martin Behaim (1492)

Behaim's globe, made in 1492 just before Columbus discovered America, does not show the New World. Even after
Columbus's voyage, however, one school of geographers
thought that the newly discovered lands were outlying
regions of Asia.

If Magellan accepted the views of this school—as some
authorities think he did—he probably took the large southeastern peninsula of Asia, shown on any Behaim-type map,
as South America. He would have considered the strait
formed at its tip by the misplacement of the Island of
Ceylon ("Seilan") there to be the strait he was looking for.
The "Aurea Chersonesus" is the Malay Peninsula, near
which the Moluccas were expected to be found.

Presumably Pigafetta's statement (page 76) that Magellan
found his strait "depicted on a map . . made by . . . Martin Behaim" refers to a map, or to a globe, of the type
shown above.

(Martin Behaim, traveller and first great German geographer, made the earliest known globe. It is still preserved in
Nuremberg, Germany.)

Globe made by Johann Schöner (1515)

Schöner's globe, made in 1515, does show the New World and represents the views of a more up-to-date school of geographers. Although he makes it much too narrow, Schöner does not call the Pacific Ocean the "Great Gulf" (as if it were an Asian bay) but the "Orientalis Oceanus" (Eastern Ocean)—and he places it between America and Asia.

Note that Schöner's globe depicts an imaginary "strait" leading from the Atlantic to the Pacific at 45° south latitude, between the land masses he labelled "America" and "Brasilie". The true strait which Magellan found lies at the bottom of South America, at 52° south latitude. Schöner based his globe in part on information given him about an earlier Portuguese voyage to South America backed by Cristóbal de Haro.

Did de Haro tell Magellan that a strait had already been found, and give him directions for reaching it? Or is the "strait" depicted by Schöner only the broad La Plata estuary? No one knows, but scholars doubt that there was definite knowledge of the strait prior to Magellan's voyage.

(Johann Schöner was a famous geographer and professor of mathematics in Nuremberg, in the sixteenth century.)

route he proposed to take, saying that the strait was left purposely blank so that no one should anticipate him.

And on that day [March, 1518] and at that hour I was in the office of the High Chancellor (Chièvres) when the Bishop of Burgos [Fonseca] brought the globe and showed the High Chancellor the voyage which was proposed; and, speaking with Magellan, I asked him what way he planned to take, and he answered that he intended to go by Cape Saint Mary, which we call the Rio de la Plata, and from thence to follow up the coast until he hit upon the strait.

But suppose you do not find any strait by which you can go into the other sea? I asked. He replied that, if he did not find any strait, he would go the way the Portuguese took [around Africa]. . . .

This Ferdinand Magellan must have been a man of courage, valiant in both his thoughts and in undertaking great things, although he was not of imposing presence, since he was small in stature and did not appear to be much.

THE KING'S ORDERS

It is a wonderful thing to have a friend, someone whose admiration you are sure of, someone to lean on. In the eighteen-year-old king of Spain, the pale, red-haired youth soon to be elected Holy Roman Emperor Charles V, Ferdinand Magellan had at last found a friend. As a boy, Charles had liked to play quietly alone with clocks and scientific instruments or to pore over maps, yet he had also excelled in sports. Now in the veteran navigator Magellan he saw someone very different from the courtiers who surrounded him, someone more like the heroic man of action he had dreamed of being.

So Charles gave Magellan his loyal support. When Bishop Fonseca had the number of Portuguese seamen Magellan was permitted to take drastically reduced, Charles, with a lordly gesture, quadrupled the number whom, he said, "We" (he and Magellan) would sign on. When the captain of one of the ships, a creature of Fonseca's, was insolent to Magellan, Charles sent him a rebuke that chilled that captain's blood. "Magellan is to choose his men," wrote Charles, making it clear that Magellan was in command.

In the contract below, Charles granted Magellan and his partner, Faleiro, very generous terms, including one fifth of the net profits of the expedition and a monopoly for exploring the westward passage for Spain for the next ten years. Magellan and Faleiro were to be made viceroys of all lands they discovered.

March 22, 1518

Since you, Ruy Faleiro and Ferdinand Magellan, knights of Portugal, wish to enter My service, I commission you to seek, in that part of the ocean which is under Our sovereignty, islands, mainlands, spices, and other things by means of which We shall be advantaged and which will benefit Our land. Therefore do I enter with you into the following contract:

You shall with good fortune voyage upon the ocean and go in search of discoveries within Our demarcation. Since it would be unjust that others should cross your path, and since you take the labours of this undertaking upon yourselves, it is therefore My will and I promise that, during the next ten years, I will give no one permission to go in quest of discoveries on the same route and in the same regions as yourselves. . . .

You must so conduct this voyage of discovery that you do not encroach upon the demarcation and boundaries of the King of Portugal. . . . For the services which you render Us, for the aggrandizement of the royal power, for the labours and dangers which you assume, you shall receive as reward the twentieth part of the proceeds and gains from all the lands and islands that you will have discovered, and shall besides receive the title of Viceroys of these lands and islands for your sons and heirs for all time. . . .

That you may be still further recompensed, it is moreover Our command that of the islands which you will have discovered, after six of them have been selected for Us, you may choose two from the remainder, of whose income and profit you shall have a fifth part, after deduction of costs.

To demonstrate Our favour, it is Our will, inasmuch as We recognize the great expenditure of money and labour which this voyage will entail upon you and since We wish to recompense you therefore, that of the net profits which you bring Us you shall have a fifth part, after deduction of the costs of the fleet.

And so that you may the better be able to consummate the above-mentioned project and the enterprise have the needed certainty of success, I declare that I promise to outfit for you five ships: two each of 130 tons, two each of 90 tons, and one of 60 tons; equipped with crew, food, and weapons for two years, including 234 men, with the captains, able seamen, and ordinary seamen necessary for the operation of the fleet, and with whatever other persons are needed. . . .

This I promise you and I give you My royal word that I shall protect you according to the above, and to this end I give you this signature of My name in Valladolid on March 22, 1518.

I, the King.

By order of the King.

ENEMY FROM PORTUGAL

In getting ready to sail, Magellan had many problems but none bigger than Dom Sebastian Alvarez, the Portuguese consul in Seville. Alvarez had been given one simple commission by his master, King Manuel of Portugal: stop Magellan. Sabotage, interception of the fleet at sea by a Portuguese fleet, or murder of Magellan—all methods were considered. In the end Alvarez achieved his greatest success through sabotage, causing a food shortage that led to starvation in the Pacific.

In the letter below, to King Manuel, Alvarez reports his unsuccessful efforts to persuade Magellan to give up the voyage, rumours about the plotting of Bishop Fonseca against Magellan, the approaching insanity of Magellan's astronomer partner, Faleiro, and details about the size, condition, cargo, and course of the ships. He concludes with the pious and patriotic wish that Magellan's expedition will go straight to the bottom of the ocean and never

be heard of again—like the Cortereal brothers, two Portuguese explorers whose ships disappeared off the North
American coast in 1501 and 1502.

Seville
July 18, 1519

Sire. . . .

There have now arrived together in this city,
Cristóbal de Haro and Juan de Cartagena, the chief
factor of the fleet and captain of a ship, and the treas-
urer and clerk of this fleet; and in the regulations
which they bring there are clauses contrary to the instructions of Ferdinand Magellan; these having been
seen by the accountant and factors of the House of
Trade, they seek how they can embroil the affairs of
Magellan, and they [the accountant and factors]
were at once of the opinion of those who have recently
arrived. . . .

And they said to him [Magellan] that he carried
many Portuguese, and that it was not well that he
should take so many. He answered, that he would do
what he chose in the fleet without giving them any
account, and that they could not do it without ren-
dering account to him. There passed between them
so many and such evil words, that the factors ordered
pay to be issued to the seamen and men-at-arms, but
not to any of the Portuguese whom Magellan and
Ruy Faleiro have got to take with them: and at the
same time a courier was sent [by the factors] to the
Court of Castile.

As I saw the matter was begun and the season con-
venient for saying that which your Highness bade
me say, I went to the lodgings of Magellan, where I
found him arranging baskets and boxes with victuals
of conserves and other things. I pressed him, feigning,
that as I found him thus occupied, it seemed to me
that the undertaking of his evil design was settled,
and that, as this would be the last conversation I
should have with him, I wished to recall to his mem-
ory how many times, as a good Portuguese and his
friend, I had spoken to him, and opposed the great
error which he was committing. . . .

He wondered much at my knowing so much, and
here he told me the truth, and that the courier had
left; all which I knew. And he told me that certainly
there would be no reason for his throwing over the
undertaking, unless they deprived him of anything
which had been assigned him by the contract. But
first he had to see what your Highness would do.

I said to him . . . that he thought he was going
as captain-major, whilst I knew that others were sent
in opposition, whom he would not know of except at
a time when he could not remedy his honour; and that
he should not pay attention to the honey, which the
Bishop of Burgos [Fonseca] put to his lips . . . and
that he should give me a letter for your Highness, and
that I from affection for him would go to your Highness to act on his behalf. . . .

He said to me that he would not say anything to me

until he saw the message which the courier brought: and with this we concluded. I will watch the service of your Highness to the full extent of my power. . . .

I spoke to Ruy Faleiro on two occasions. He never answered me anything else than, how could he do anything against the king his lord, who did him such favour. To all that I said to him, he did not reply anything else. It seems to me that he is like a man deranged in his senses, and that . . . if Ferdinand Magellan were removed, that Ruy Faleiro would follow whatever Magellan did.

The ships of Magellan's fleet, Sire, are five; that is to say, one of 110 tons, two of 80 tons each, and the other two of 60 tons each, a little more or less. They are very old and patched up; for I saw them when they were beached for repairs. It is eleven months since they were repaired, and they are now afloat, and they are caulking them in the water. I went on board of them a few times, and I assure your Highness that I should be ill inclined to sail in them to the Canaries, because their knees [wooden braces supporting the ship's timbers] are of touchwood [rotten].

The artillery which they all carry are eighty guns, of a very small size; only in the largest ship, in which Magellan is going, there are four very good iron cannon. All the crews whom they take in all the five vessels are 230 men. The greater number have already received their pay; only the Portuguese, who will not accept a thousand reis, and who are waiting for the courier to arrive, because Magellan told them that he would get their pay increased, and they carry provisions for two years.

The "thousand reis" the Portuguese would not accept was their monthly pay   less than three pounds.

The captain of the first ship is Ferdinand Magellan, and of the second, Ruy Faleiro; of the third, Juan de Cartagena, who is the chief factor of the fleet; of the fourth, Quesada, a dependent of the Archbishop of Seville; the fifth goes without any known captain—Carvalho, a Portuguese, goes in her as pilot. Here it is said that, as soon as they are out of the mouth of the river, he will put into her, as captain, Alvaro de Mesquita of Estremoz, who is here. . . .

The goods which they take are copper, quicksilver, common cloths of colours, common coloured silks, and jackets made of these silks.

It is assured that this fleet will start down the river at the end of this July; but it does not seem so to me, nor before the middle of August, even though the courier should come more quickly.

The course which it is said they are to take is straight to Cape Frio [near Rio de Janeiro], Brazil remaining on their right hand, until they reach the line of the demarcation; from thence they are to navigate to the west and west-north-west, straight to Maluco [the Moluccas]. . . .

From this Cape Frio, until the islands of Maluco

throughout this navigation, there are no lands laid down in the maps which they carry with them. Please God the Almighty that they may make such a voyage as did the Cortereals, and that your Highness may be at rest, and forever be envied, as you are, by all princes. . . .

Sebastian Alvarez

MAGELLAN'S WILL

Less than a month before he sailed Magellan made his will. Although members of the fleet were enjoying a gay round of last-minute parties, few could forget that this shore was "one of tears for those who left and of joy for those who returned." One third of Vasco da Gama's men, for example, had perished on the first voyage around Africa to India.

The bequests in Magellan's will reveal his character: devout, responsible, proud of his name and position. First, he gives directions for his burial, for donations to hospitals and churches, and for the ransom of Christian captives of the Moors. Next, he provides in more than one article for his wife, Lady Beatriz, and their son, Rodrigo. Finally, he frees his one slave, the faithful Enrique de Malacca (Henry of Malacca).

Since the will is a long document, only a few items are printed below as examples. Magellan, Lady Beatriz, and Rodrigo all died within three years; none of the provisions was carried out.

August 24, 1519

Know all ye by these presents, that I, Ferdinand Magellan, Commander, His Majesty's Captain-general of the Armada bound for the Spice Islands, husband of Doña Beatriz Barbosa, and inhabitant of this most noble and most loyal city of Seville. . . .

Whereas I am about to proceed in the King's service in the said Armada, by these presents I make known and declare that I make and ordain this my Will. . . .

Firstly, I commend my soul to God our Lord, who made and created it, and redeemed me with His precious blood. . . . And when this my present life shall end for the life eternal, I desire that if I die in this city of Seville my body may be buried in the Monastery of Santa Maria de la Victoria in Triana—ward and precinct of this city of Seville—in the grave set apart for me; And if I die in this said voyage, I desire that my body may be buried in a church dedicated to Our Lady, in the nearest spot to that at which death seize me. . . .

And I bequeath to the Orders of the Holy Trinity and Santa Maria de la Merced of this city of Seville, in aid of the redemption of such faithful Christians as may be captives in the country of the Moors, the enemies of our holy Catholic faith, to each Order a real of silver. . . .

And I desire that upon the said day of my burial three poor men may be clothed—such as I have indicated to my executors—and that to each may be given a cloak of gray stuff, a cap, a shirt, and a pair of shoes, that they may pray to God for my soul. . . .

And I confess . . . that I received and obtained
in dowry and marriage with the said Doña Beatriz
Barbosa, my wife, six hundred thousand maravedis
. . . and I desire that before everything the said
Doña Beatriz Barbosa, my wife, may be paid and put
in possession of the said six hundred thousand maravedis, her dowry, together with the arras that I gave
her. . . .

And . . . I declare and ordain as free and quit of
every obligation of captivity, subjection, and slavery,
my captured slave Enrique, mulatto, native of the
city of Malacca, of the age of twenty-six years more
or less, that from the day of my death thenceforward
for ever the said Enrique may be free . . . and I
desire that of my estate there may be given to the said
Enrique the sum of ten thousand maravedis in money
for his support; and this manumission I grant because
he is a Christian, and that he may pray to God for my
soul. . . .

A maravedi was less than a penny. Enrique's ten thousand maravedis would amount to about thirty pounds; the
Lady Beatriz's six hundred thousand maravedis, to about
two thousand pounds.

I desire that all and everything of the said possessions which may remain over and above may be had
and inherited by the said Rodrigo Magellan, my legiti-
mate son by the said Doña Beatriz, my wife, and by

the child or children of which the said Doña Beatriz
is now pregnant . . . And if, which may God for-
bid, the said my son, or child borne by my wife, die
before attaining the proper age for the succession, I
desire that the said Doña Beatriz Barbosa, my wife,
may inherit the said my estate. . . .

Done in Seville, in the King's Customs of this city
of Seville, Wednesday, the 24th day of the month of
August, in the year of the birth of our Saviour Jesus
Christ 1519.

CHAPTER TWO

ACROSS THE ATLANTIC

August 10, 1519 — December 26, 1519

In Brazil . . . there are many rivers and ports. . . . In this bay [Rio de Janeiro Bay] there are good people, and plenty of them, and they go naked, and barter [for] fishhooks, and looking-glasses, and little bells, [with] victuals. There is a good deal of brazil wood, and this bay is in 23° [south latitude], and we entered here the day of St. Lucy [December 13].

—The Log-Book of Francisco Albo

A REPORTER JOINS THE FLEET

"I presented to his sacred Majesty, Charles V, neither gold nor silver," said Antonio Pigafetta after his return to Spain in the *Victoria*, "but things very highly esteemed by such a sovereign. Among other things I gave him a book, written by my hand, concerning all the matters that had occurred from day to day during our voyage."

Indeed, the thirty-year-old Venetian nobleman had had an experience that all the kings and scholars of Europe were eager to share. He had sailed around the world with Magellan.

Three years earlier, in 1519, Antonio had been an obscure gentleman-in-waiting to the pope's representative at the Spanish court. His keen eye swept the throngs of courtiers, noting the follies and the scandals. But Antonio also had a dream, about the new lands discovered in the great Ocean Sea—the Atlantic and other oceans—thought of as surrounding the inhabited earth. What were these lands like? What kind of people lived in them? While still a boy, according to one story, Antonio had run away to sail the Mediterranean in one of the galleys of the Knights of Rhodes.

Now he impulsively asked permission of the papal nuncio and King Charles to enlist with Magellan as a supernumerary, a gentleman volunteer. Permission was granted, and Antonio arrived in Seville with his observant eye and open notebook. So the fleet gained a reporter.

Don Antonio Lombardo (Antonio the Lombard), as Pigafetta was called on the cruise, was interested in everything around him. Strange birds and fish, mysterious lights at sea, the dress and appearance of Indian men and women, their homes and tools, cannibalism—he described it all. And as Antonio stood on the heaving deck of the *Trinidad*, forging slowly west under sails painted with the red cross of Santiago, he probably thought of every man's last voyage, also into the unknown, signed with the cross of Christ. ("Santiago" means "St. James"; St. James was the patron saint of Spain, and his name was the battle cry of Spanish troops.)

Shortly after his return to Spain Antonio Pigafetta wrote a more finished work, based on his day-to-day journal—one of the best accounts of an early voyage, also the most moving description of the death of Magellan, whom he loved. He returned to Europe to tell his story at the courts of Spain, Portugal, and France, and before the council of Venice—then retired from the world as a member of the religious-military order of the Knights of Rhodes. He died in 1536 while fighting to defend Malta against the Turks. A condensation of his book was published in Paris in 1525, but the complete manuscript was not printed until the nineteenth century. An excellent English translation was made by James A. Robertson in 1906.

We will be reading much of Pigafetta's narrative (the Robertson translation) in this book, with a few passages introduced from other sources for additional facts. Unless otherwise stated, the selections which follow are from Pigafetta.

Antonio Pigafetta, patrician of Venice and Knight of Rhodes, to the most illustrious and excellent Lord, Philippe Villiers l'Ile-Adam, renowned grand master of Rhodes, his most honoured lord.

Inasmuch as, most illustrious and excellent Lord, there are many curious persons who not only take pleasure in knowing and hearing the great and wonderful things which God has permitted me to see and suffer during my long and dangerous voyage . . . but who also wish to know the means and manners

and paths that I have taken in making that voyage
. . . therefore, your most illustrious Lordship must
know that, finding myself, in the year of the nativity
of our Saviour 1519 in Spain, in the court of the most
serene king of the Romans [Charles V] . . . I determined, by the good favour of his Caesarean Majesty
[Charles V] . . . to experience and to go to see those
things for myself, so that I might be able thereby to
satisfy myself somewhat, and so that I might be able
to gain some renown for later posterity.

Having heard that a fleet composed of five vessels
had been fitted out in the city of Seville for the purpose of going to discover the spicery in the islands of
Maluco [the Moluccas], under command of Captain-
general Ferdinand Magellan . . . I set out from the
city of Barcelona, where his Majesty was then resid-
ing, bearing many letters in my favour. I went by ship
as far as Malaga, where, taking the highroad, I went
overland to Seville.

Having been there about three full months [June,
July, August, 1519], waiting for the said fleet to be
set in order for the departure, finally . . . we com-
menced our voyage under most happy auspices. And
inasmuch as when I was in Italy . . . you . . . told
me that you would be greatly pleased if I would
write down for you all those things which I had seen
and suffered during my voyage . . . I offer you, in
this little book of mine, all my vigils, hardships, and
wanderings.

C

FOLLOW THE *FAROL*

Magellan's fleet consisted of five *naos*. *Nao* is a Spanish word meaning "ship." It was used specifically for a cumbersome, round-bellied merchant ship, a slow vessel about one-third as broad as it was long. Magellan's five naos were seaworthy and strong after he repaired them, but not as trim as the caravels in which he had sailed the Indian Ocean.

The caravel was a long, relatively light vessel with one or more lateen sails. The lateen (from "Latin," that is, Mediterranean) sail was three-cornered and enabled the caravel to sail against the wind. This rig was borrowed from the Arabs. At first caravels carried lateen sails on three masts, but later the *caravela redonda*, a caravel with square sails on foremast and mainmast and lateen sail only at the stern, was found better for ocean voyages. Columbus' *Santa Maria* was a nao, but his favourite, *Niña*, was a *caravela redonda*. Crack French airliners today are called Caravelles.

The names of Magellan's ships were the *San Antonio* (120 tons, over fifty men), the *Trinidad* (110 tons, over sixty men), the *Concepción* (90 tons, over forty men), the *Victoria* (85 tons, over forty men), and the *Santiago* (75 tons, over thirty men). Their size is given in "tons," that is, the number of "tuns" or casks of wine that each could carry. The ton was roughly equivalent to 40 cubic feet. The *San Antonio* would be listed at about 143 tons today, and the other ships' tonnage increased proportionately.

The *San Antonio* and *Trinidad* would have been slightly larger than Columbus' *Santa Maria*, which is thought to have had the following measurements: length from stem to stern, 78½ feet; length of keel, 55½ feet; breadth, 26 feet. Magellan's three other ships were smaller.

These naos each had a single main deck, which rose to

a high forecastle at the front and sterncastle at the rear. Antonio Pigafetta and the crew stowed their chests and blanket rolls in the low waist of the ship, on the open main deck, which meant these belongings were always wet with spray. In a storm Antonio would seek shelter in the storage rooms of the forecastle or on the low-ceilinged gun deck just below the main deck. The gun deck was not much more than a shelf running around the wide hatch, or opening, descending into the ship's dark hold with its sloshing bilge water.

The chief officers of a sixteenth century Spanish ship were the "captain"—really the commanding officer, hence usually a nobleman—responsible for discipline, morale, and the success of the venture though he was not necessarily a seaman; the "master," an experienced seaman in charge of sailing the ship and thus corresponding to our idea of a captain; and the "pilot," in charge of navigation and corresponding to our first mate.

The *farol*, or lantern, used for the signals described here was displayed on the roof of the sterncastle, the ship's poop. Actually, the farol was an iron cage in which firewood was burned at night.

The captain-general having resolved to make so long a voyage through the Ocean Sea, where furious winds and great storms are always reigning, but not desiring to make known to any of his men the voyage that he was about to make, so that they might not be cast down at the thought of doing so great and extraordinary a deed as he did accomplish with the aid of God (the captains who accompanied him hated him exceedingly, I know not why, unless because he was a Portuguese, and they Spaniards) . . . prescribed the following orders and gave them to all the pilots and masters of his ships, so that the ships might not become separated from one another during the storms and night.

These were to the effect that he would always precede the other ships at night, and they were to follow his ship which would have a large torch of wood, which they call *farol*. He always carried that *farol* set at the poop of his ship as a signal so that they might always follow him. Another light was made by means of a lantern or by means of a piece of wicking made from a rush and called *sparto* rope which is well beaten in the water, and then dried in the sun or in the smoke—a most excellent material for such use. They were to answer him so that he might know by that signal whether all of the ships were coming together.

If he showed two lights besides that of the *farol*, they were to veer or take another tack, doing this when the wind was not favourable or suitable for us to continue on our way, or when he wished to sail slowly. If he showed three lights, they were to lower away the bonnet sail, which is a part of the sail that is fastened below the mainsail, when the weather is suitable for making better time. It is lowered so that it may be easier to furl the mainsail when it is struck hastily during a sudden squall. If he showed four lights, they were to strike all the sails; after which he showed a signal by one light, which meant that he was standing still.

If he showed a greater number of lights, or fired a mortar, it was a signal of land or of shoals. Then he showed four lights when he wished to have the sails set full, so that they might always sail in his wake by the torch on the poop. When he desired to set the bonnet sail, he showed three lights. When he desired to alter his course, he showed two; and then if he wished to ascertain whether all the ships were following and whether they were coming together, he showed one light, so that each one of the ships might do the same and reply to him.

Three watches were set nightly: the first at the beginning of the night; the second, which is called the midnight, and the third at the end of the night. All of the men in the ships were divided into three parts: the first was the division of the captain or boatswain, those two alternating nightly; the second, of either the pilot or boatswain's mate; and the third, of the master. Thus did the captain-general order that all the ships observe the above signals and watches, so that their voyage might be more propitious.

DEPARTURE FROM SEVILLE

On Monday morning, August 10, [1519], St. Lawrence's day, the fleet, having been supplied with all the things necessary for the sea (and counting those of every nationality, we were 237 men), made

Sailing ships in the
Atlantic encounter
a shoal of flying fish

(From De Bry's
Americae III, 1592)

ready to leave the harbour of Seville. Discharging many pieces of artillery, the ships held their forestaysails to the wind, and descended the river Betis, at present called Guadalquivir, passing by a village called San Juan de Aznalfarache, once a large Moorish settlement.

In the midst of it was once a bridge that crossed the said river, and led to Seville. Two columns of that bridge have remained even to this day at the bottom of the water, and when ships sail by there, they need men who know the location of the columns thoroughly, so that the ships may not strike against them. They must also be passed when the river is highest with the tide. . . .

Then the ships reached another village called Coria, and passed by many other villages along the river, until they came to a castle of the duke of Medina Sidonia, called San Lúcar, which is a port by which to enter the Ocean Sea. It is in an east and west direction with the cape of St. Vincent, which lies in thirty-seven degrees of latitude, and ten leagues from the said port. From Seville to this point [San Lúcar], it is seventeen or twenty leagues by river. Some days after, the captain-general, with his other captains, descended the river in the small boats belonging to their ships.

We remained there for a considerable number of days in order to finish providing the fleet with some things that it needed. Every day we went ashore to hear mass in a village called Nostra Dona de Barrameda, near San Lúcar. Before the departure, the captain-general wished all the men to confess. . . .

We left . . . San Lúcar on Tuesday, September 20, [1519] and took a south-west course. On the 26th of the said month, we reached an island of the Canaries, called Tenerife, which lies in a latitude of twenty-eight degrees, landing there in order to get flesh, water, and wood. We stayed there for three and one-half days in order to furnish the fleet with the said supplies. Then we went to a port of the same island called Monte Rosso to get pitch, staying there two days.

Your most illustrious Lordship must know that there is a particular one of the islands of the Canaries, where one can not find a single drop of water which gushes up from a spring; but that at noontide a cloud descends from the sky and encircles a large tree which grows in the said island, the leaves and branches of which distil a quantity of water. At the foot of the said tree runs a trench which resembles a spring, where all the water falls, and from which the people living there, and the animals, both domestic and wild, fully satisfy themselves daily with this water and no other.

This story of a rain-giving tree is found in ancient Roman writings about the Canary Islands and has a basis in fact. The daily mists are so heavy that the laurel and other heavily foliaged trees condense water and drip constantly.

A WARNING

While the fleet was in the Canary Islands Magellan's father-in-law sent him a warning of the plot of the three Spanish ship captains against him. When the fleet sailed from the Canary Islands, Juan Cartagena, the captains' ringleader, questioned the course Magellan was taking.

"Your orders are to follow my flag by day and my lantern by night," Magellan said sternly, and the opposition collapsed—for the time being.

The episode of the warning is narrated by the Portuguese historian Corrêa, who served in India under Albuquerque. The passage below is from Corrêa's *Lendas da India*—"Legends" or "Records" of India, a history of Portuguese Asia, written 1530–63.

Whilst [Magellan] was there [in the Canary Islands] a vessel arrived with letters from his father-in-law, in which he warned him to keep a good watch for his personal safety, because he had learned that the captains whom he took with him had said to their friends and relations, that if he annoyed them they would kill him, and would rise up against him.

To this he replied, that he would do them no injuries [that would give them] reason to act thus; [furthermore, not he but the overseers had appointed them]; and whether they were good or bad, he would labour to do the service of the emperor, and for that they had offered their lives. The father-in-law showed this answer to the overseers [board of directors of the House of Trade of the Indies], who greatly praised the good heart of Magellan.

WINDS, CALMS, AND RAINS

After leaving the Canaries, Magellan crossed the Atlantic, the "Sea of Darkness and Mystery," on a diagonal south-south-west course, striking the coast of Brazil just below Cape Roque, close to its easternmost point. First, however, he played hide-and-seek with a Portuguese fleet which King Manuel sent to intercept him. That is why he sailed into the doldrums, the area of dead calm, off the coast of Guinea, Africa. The Portuguese didn't think of looking here and eventually gave up the search. After twenty-one days of heat and drenching rains, Magellan's ships drifted into the area of the south-east trade winds, which then blew them across the Atlantic.

A storm off Sierra Leone, Africa, proved the greatest danger to the fleet. The rounded merchant naos heeled over so far that their yardarms dipped into the sea, while Pigafetta and the crews clung together on the forecastles, weeping and praying. At last the "holy body, that is to say St. Elmo," shone on the mastheads, and the storm lessened. These blue lights, which the sailors considered supernatural, were star-shaped discharges of the electricity in the atmosphere.

"St. Elmo" is St. Erasmus ("Elmo" is derived from "Erasmus"), a fourth-century Italian bishop and martyr who became the patron saint of sailors. "St. Elmo's Fire" was believed sent by the saint to show his protection and as a sign that a storm was lessening. Magellan's men were comforted by these lights more than once during their voyage.

On the crossing Captain Juan Cartagena again became rebellious. When he declared that he would not obey Magellan's orders, Magellan removed the proud Spaniard from his command and placed him in a pair of wooden stocks on the forecastle of the *Trinidad*.

Pigafetta's narrative continues below.

At midnight of Monday, October 3, [1519], the sails were trimmed toward the south, and we took to the open Ocean Sea, passing between Cape Verde and its islands in fourteen and one-half degrees [north latitude]. Thus for many days did we sail along the coast of Guinea . . . where there is a mountain called Sierra Leone, which lies in eight degrees of [north] latitude, with contrary winds, calms, and rains without wind, until we reached the equinoctial line [the equator], having sixty days of continual rain.

Contrary to the opinion of the ancients, before we reached the line many furious squalls of wind, and currents of water struck us head on in fourteen degrees [north latitude]. As we could not advance, and in order that the ships might not be wrecked, all the sails were struck; and in this manner did we wander hither and yon on the sea, waiting for the tempest to cease, for it was very furious. When it rained there was no wind. When the sun shone, it was calm.

Certain large fishes called *tiburoni* [sharks] came to the side of the ships. They have terrible teeth, and whenever they find men in the sea they devour them. We caught many of them with iron hooks, although they are not good to eat unless they are small, and even then they are not very good.

During those storms the holy body, that is to say St. Elmo, appeared to us many times, in light—among other times on an exceedingly dark night, with the brightness of a blazing torch, on the maintop, where he stayed for about two hours or more, to our consolation, for we were weeping. When that blessed light was about to leave us, so dazzling was the brightness that it cast into our eyes, that we all remained for more than an eighth of an hour blinded and calling for mercy. And truly when we thought that we were dead men, the sea suddenly grew calm.

I saw many kinds of birds, among them one that . . . when the female wishes to lay its eggs, it does so on the back of the male and there they are hatched. . . . I also saw many flying fish, and many others collected together, so that they resembled an island.

THE NATIVES OF BRAZIL

Magellan's first stop in the New World was on the warm, humid coast of Brazil. ("Brazil" takes its name from a special kind of wood, brazilwood, from which a red dye is obtained.) Here, on the site of Rio de Janeiro (River of January), so named from the month in which it was discovered earlier, Magellan's men secured fresh water, food, and rest. They found the weather hot in December because in the southern hemisphere the seasons are reversed, summer coming at the time of our winter, autumn at the time of our spring, and so on. Magellan sailed this far south before landing to avoid the hostile Portuguese settlements to the north.

Just as the fleet arrived, a two months' drought came to an end. Hence the Indians looked upon the white men as gods who had brought the rain. Since Magellan did not abuse or enslave the Indians, the thirteen-day stay was peaceful and Pigafetta had opportunity to make many observations. His story of how these Guaraní Indians became cannibals is a "tall tale," based on hearsay, but his comments about their appearance, food, houses, and language are accurate.

After we had passed the equinoctial line [the equator] going south, we lost the north star, and hence we sailed south south-west until we reached a land called the land of Brazil. . . . There we got a plentiful refreshment of fowls, potatoes, many sweet pineapples—in truth the most delicious fruit that can be found—the flesh of the *anta* [tapir], which resembles beef, sugar cane, and innumerable other things, which I shall not mention in order not to be prolix.

For one fishhook or one knife, those people gave five or six chickens; for one comb, a brace of geese; for one mirror or one pair of scissors, as many fish as would be sufficient for ten men; for a bell or one leather lace, one basketful of potatoes. These potatoes resemble chestnuts in taste, and are as long as turnips. For a king of diamonds which is a playing card, they gave me six fowls and thought that they had even cheated me.

We entered that port on St. Lucy's day [December 13, 1519], and on that day had the sun on the zenith; and we were subjected to greater heat on that day and on the other days when we had the sun on the zenith, than when we were under the equinoctial line.

That land of Brazil is wealthier and larger than Spain, France, and Italy, put together, and belongs to the king of Portugal. The people of that land are not Christians, and have no manner of worship. They live according to the dictates of nature, and reach an age of one hundred and twenty-five and one hundred and forty years. They go naked, both men and women. They live in certain long houses which they call *boii*, and sleep in cotton *hamacas* [hammocks], which are fastened in those houses by each end to large beams. A fire is built on the ground under those hammocks. In each one of those *boii*, there are one hundred men with their wives and children, and they make a great racket.

They have boats called canoes made of one single huge tree, hollowed out by the use of stone hatchets. Those people employ stones as we do iron, as they have no iron. Thirty or forty men occupy one of those boats. They paddle with blades like the shovels of a furnace, and thus, black, naked, and shaven, they

Line of
Demarcation 1494

Japan

Ryukyu Islands

iu
oa
anore
Calicut
Cochin

Iadia

Siam

Formosa

Philippines

Guam (Ladrones)

Ceylon

Malacca

Borneo

Sumatra

Moluccas

Timor

New Guinea

Australia

Amsterdam Island

Pacific Ocean

Portuguese Hemisphere

Spanish Hemisphere

The route of the voyage around the world

resemble, when paddling, the inhabitants of the Stygian marsh. Men and women are as well proportioned as we.

They eat the human flesh of their enemies, not because it is good, but because it is a certain established custom. That custom, which is mutual, was begun by an old woman, who had but one son who was killed by his enemies. In return some days later, that old woman's friends captured one of the company who had killed her son, and brought him to the place of her abode. She seeing him, and remembering her son, ran upon him . . . and bit him on one shoulder.

Shortly afterward he escaped to his own people, whom he told that they had tried to eat him, showing them in proof the marks on his shoulder. Whomever the latter captured afterward at any time from the former they ate, and the former did the same to the latter, so that such a custom has sprung up in this way.

They do not eat the bodies all at once, but everyone cuts off a piece, and carries it to his house, where he smokes it. Then every week, he cuts off a small bit, which he eats thus smoked with his other food to remind him of his enemies. The above was told me by the pilot, Juan Carvalho, who came with us, and who had lived in that land for four years.

Those people paint the whole body and the face in

a wonderful manner with fire in various fashions, as do the women also. The men are smooth shaven and have no beard, for they pull it out. They clothe themselves in a dress made of parrot feathers. . . . Almost all the people, except the women and children, have three holes pierced in the lower lip, where they carry round stones, one finger or thereabouts in length and hanging down outside.

Those people are not entirely black, but of a dark brown colour. . . . Both men and women always go naked. Their king is called cacique. They have an infinite number of parrots, and gave us eight or ten for one mirror; and little monkeys that look like lions, only they are yellow, and very beautiful. They make round, white loaves of bread from the marrowy substance of trees, which is not very good, and is found between the wood and the bark and resembles buttermilk curds. They have swine which have their navels on their backs, and large birds with beaks like spoons and no tongues.

The men gave us one or two of their young daughters as slaves for one hatchet or one large knife, but they would not give us their wives in exchange for anything at all. . . .

The women cultivate the fields, and carry all their food from the mountains in panniers or baskets on the head or fastened to the head. But they are always accompanied by their husbands, who are armed only

with a bow of brazilwood or of black palmwood, and
a bundle of cane arrows, doing this because they are
jealous of their wives. The women carry their children hanging in a cotton net from their necks. I omit
other particulars, in order not to be tedious.

Mass was said twice on shore, during which those
people remained on their knees with so great contrition and with clasped hands raised aloft, that it was
an exceeding great pleasure to behold them. They
built us a house as they thought that we were going
to stay with them for some time, and at our departure
they cut a great quantity of brazilwood to give us.

It had been about two months since it had rained
in that land, and when we reached that port, it happened to rain, whereupon they said that we came
from the sky and that we had brought the rain with
us. Those people could be converted easily to the faith
of Jesus Christ.

At first those people thought that the small boats
were the children of the ships, and that the latter gave
birth to them when they were lowered into the sea
from the ships, and when they were lying so alongside
the ships (as is the custom), they believed that the
ships were nursing them. . . .

Some words of those people of Brazil:

for Millet	maiz
for Flour	hui
for Fishhook	pinda

for Knife	tacse
for Comb	chigap
for Scissors	pirame
for Bell	itanmaraca
Good, better	tum maragathum

CHAPTER THREE

MUTINY AT ST. JULIAN

December 26, 1519 — August 24, 1520

We did not take the [altitude of the] sun again until we entered a port called St. Julian, and we entered there on the last day of March, and remained there till the day of St. Bartholomew, which is the 24th of August, and the said port is in 49 2/3° [south latitude], and there we caulked the ships, and many Indians came there, who go covered with skins of antas, which are like camels without humps.

—The Log-Book of Francisco Albo

RIVER OF CANNIBALS

From Rio de Janeiro with its setting of rocks and head-lands, of blue bays against green mountains, Magellan sailed down to the great gash in the South American coast where Buenos Aires is located today—the La Plata estuary.

The La Plata River is 138 miles wide at its mouth, 25 miles wide at its source, where it receives two other large rivers. It reaches 170 miles into the continent. No wonder Juan de Solis, exploring it a few years earlier, thought he had found the longed-for passage to the Pacific.

Magellan was confident that this was the strait. He sent the *Santiago* up it to explore while he sailed across to the low south shore, which he considered the Antarctic continent. In returning, he sighted an elevation on the north shore and called "I see a mountain!" Thus Montevideo, the present capital of Uruguay, received its name.

But the *Santiago* came back with news that this vast body of water was only a river. Magellan was bitterly disappointed. After searching both banks for three weeks, he had to face his assembled officers and crews, who wished to return to warm Brazil for the winter, and persuade them to continue south. He convinced them that the *paso* was only a short distance away, that the Spice Islands, with wealth and pleasure for all, lay just beyond.

Rio de la Plata (River of Silver) was so named a few years later by Sebastian Cabot, who saw many Indians wearing silver ornaments (which had come from the Inca Empire of Peru). Magellan's men called it Rio de Solis, after Juan de Solis, who had been ambushed and eaten by the cannibals here in 1516.

Pigafetta's narrative continues below.

[At the La Plata River] we found people . . . called cannibals, who eat human flesh. One of them, in stature almost a giant, came to the flagship in order to assure the safety of the others his friends. He had a voice like a bull.

The Indian who came to the flagship told Magellan that his tribe possessed much silver, but he went away the next day and did not return.

While he was in the ship, the others carried away their possessions from the place where they were living into the interior, for fear of us. Seeing that, we landed one hundred men in order to have speech and converse with them, or to capture one of them by force. They fled, and in fleeing they took so large a step that we although running could not gain on their steps.

There are seven islands in that river [the La Plata], in the largest of which precious gems are found. That place is called the cape of Santa Maria, and it was formerly thought that one passed thence to the Sea of Sur, that is to say the South Sea, but nothing further was ever discovered. Now the name is not given to a cape, but to a river, with a mouth seventeen leagues in width. A Spanish captain, called Juan de Solis and sixty men, who were going to discover lands like us, were formerly eaten at that river by those cannibals because of too great confidence.

SEALS AND PENGUINS

Pigafetta's "geese" below are penguins; his "seawolves," seals. Magellan had left Rio de la Plata on February 3,

1520, and was now sailing along the bleak coast of Patagonia, past the pampas ("flat country") of modern Argentina. Once a party of his men, landing on a rocky islet to kill seals and penguins for fresh meat, was cut off from the fleet overnight by a storm. They escaped freezing to death only by burying themselves under the seals they had just killed.

With March came the beginning of cold weather in the Southern Hemisphere. Antarctic gales bearing hail and sleet battered the ships, and Magellan sought winter quarters.

Then proceeding on the same course toward the Antarctic Pole, coasting along the land, we came to anchor at two islands full of geese and seawolves. Truly, the great number of those geese cannot be reckoned; in one hour we loaded the five ships with them. Those geese are black and have all their feathers alike both on body and wings. They do not fly, and live on fish. They were so fat that it was not necessary to pluck them but to skin them. Their beak is like that of a crow.

These seawolves are of various colours, and as large as a calf, with a head like that of a calf, ears small and round, and large teeth. They have no legs but only feet with small nails attached to the body, which resemble our hands, and between their fingers the same kind of skin as the geese. They would be very fierce if they could run. They swim, and live on fish. At that place the ships suffered a very great storm,

during which the three holy bodies appeared to us
many times, that is to say, St. Elmo, St. Nicholas,
and St. Clara, whereupon the storm quickly ceased.

This is another reference to the discharges of electricity
in the atmosphere, the lights around the ships' mastheads,
which the sailors attributed to the patron saints of seamen.

Leaving that place, we finally reached forty-nine
and one-half degrees toward the Antarctic Pole. As it
was winter, the ships entered a safe port to winter [on
March 31, 1520]. . . . In that port which we called
the port of St. Julian, we remained about five months.

THE MUTINEERS

Winter in St. Julian: gray skies, freezing cold, home-
sickness, and bitterness. Everyone except Magellan wished
to give up the voyage.

Again the captain-general tried to change their minds.
He explained to the crews that he had reduced their ration
of biscuit and wine only to conserve food; they could build
snug wooden barracks, catch fish and waterfowl, and live
comfortably through a few snowy months. But when he
rejected the demand of his officers that he sail back up the
coast to the La Plata River, the Spanish captains spread
rumours that he was a Portuguese spy leading the fleet to
destruction.

Magellan was clear-sighted. He suspected that the following officers were plotting against him: Quesada and
Mendoza, captains of the *Concepción* and *Victoria*, respec-
tively; Cartagena and de Coca, both former captains of the
San Antonio who had been relieved of their commands
because of disobedience; and del Cano, master of the *Concepción*. Officers loyal to Magellan included his incom-
petent cousin Mesquita, now captain of the *San Antonio*;

his very dependable cousin Juan Serrano, captain of the *Santiago*; Espinosa, chief sergeant at arms of the fleet; and Lloriaga, master of the *San Antonio*. The common seamen took neither side strongly but would have been glad to return to Spain.

On the night of Palm Sunday, April 1, 1520, the mutiny broke out. Thirty men, headed by Cartagena and Quesada, boarded the *San Antonio*, mortally wounded Lloriaga, imprisoned Captain Mesquita, and turned the ship against Magellan. Now the officers aboard the *San Antonio*, *Concepción*, and *Victoria* all refused to obey Magellan's orders. Three of his five ships, containing nearly two-thirds of his men and supplies, were captured by mutineers. His own ship, the *Trinidad*, would be attacked the next evening. The expedition seemed doomed.

Magellan was never more dangerous, however, than when faced by overwhelming odds. He pretended to negotiate with the mutineers and sent a letter by his sergeant at arms, the dauntless Espinosa, to Captain Mendoza on the *Victoria*. When Mendoza allowed Espinosa to board the ship, Espinosa stabbed him in the throat and Mendoza fell dead.

At the same moment a boat from Magellan's *Trinidad* bearing fifteen heavily armed men raced for the *Victoria*. The men swarmed over the bulwark and took the ship without another blow struck. The *Victoria* then joined the *Trinidad* and the faithful *Santiago* at the ocean entrance of St. Julian, blocking the rebels' escape.

That evening a sailor loyal to Magellan on the rebel *San Antonio* cut the ship's anchor cable. The *San Antonio* drifted down toward Magellan's three ships and was captured. Cartagena, on the *Concepción*, surrendered. The mutiny was over.

Because the revolt involved high-ranking Spaniards (such as Cartagena, who had Bishop Fonseca's backing, as well as del Cano, who brought the only surviving ship, the *Victoria*, back to Spain), the subject was a touchy one after the voyage. Pigafetta cautiously omitted almost all the details from his narrative. The account below, therefore, is taken from Corrêa's *Lendas da India*.

While they were there [at St. Julian] taking in water and wood, Juan de Cartagena, who was [formerly] sub-captain-major, agreed with the other captains to rise up, saying that Magellan had got them betrayed and entrapped.

As they understood that [Alvaro de Mesquita] was a friend of Magellan's, Juan de Cartagena got into his boat at night, with [thirty] men, and went to the ship [the *San Antonio*] of [Alvaro de Mesquita], and went in to speak to him, and took him prisoner, and made a relation of his captain of the ship, in order that all three might go at once to board Magellan and kill him, and after that they would reduce the other ship [the *Santiago*] of Juan Serrano, and would take the money and goods, which they would hide, and would return to the emperor, and would tell him that Magellan had got them entrapped and deceived, having broken faith with his instructions, since he was navigating in seas and countries of the King of Portugal: for which deed they would get first a safe conduct from the emperor. So they arranged matters for their treason, which turned out ill for them.

Magellan had some suspicion of this matter, and

before this should happen, he sent his skiff to the ships to tell the captains that the masters were to arrange their ships for beaching them to [overhaul] them; and with this pretext he warned a servant of his to notice what the captains answered. When this skiff came to the revolted ships they did not let it come alongside, saying that they would not execute any orders except those of Juan de Cartagena, who was their captain-major.

The skiff having returned with this answer, Magellan spoke to [Gomez de Espinosa], his chief constable, a valiant man, and gave him orders what he was to do, and to go secretly armed; and he sent a letter to Luís de Mendoza by him, with six men in the skiff, whom the chief constable selected. And the current set towards the ships, and Magellan ordered his master to bend a long hawser, with which he might drop down to the ships if it suited him.

"To bend a long hawser" meant to fasten an extra length of rope to the anchor, so that when the rope was paid out the current, which had set towards the mutinous ships, would carry Magellan's ships alongside them. This was a common stratagem for surprising a nearby ship.

All being thus arranged, the skiff went . . . alongside [the *Victoria*] of Luís de Mendoza, [who] would not let [Espinosa] come on board. So the chief constable said to the captain that it was weakness not to bid him enter, as he was one man alone who was bringing a letter. Upon which the captain bade him enter. He came on board, and giving him the letter, took him in his arms, shouting: "On behalf of the emperor, you are arrested!"

At this the men of the skiff came on board with their swords drawn; then the chief constable cut the throat of Luís de Mendoza with a dagger, for he held him thrown down under him, for so Magellan had given him orders. Upon this a tumult arose, and Magellan hearing it, ordered the hawser to be paid out, and with his ship dropped down upon the other ships, with his men under arms, and the artillery in readiness.

On reaching the ship [the *Victoria*] of Mendoza . . . he at once made captain Duarte Barbosa, a Portuguese, and a friend of his: and he ordered the corpse of Mendoza to be hung up by the feet, that they might see him from the other ships.

He then ordered Barbosa to prepare the men for going and boarding one of the other ships; . . . he . . . spoke secretly to a sailor, whom he trusted, who fled to the ship [the *San Antonio*] of [Quesada], where, at night when the current set for Magellan's ship, which was astern, the sailor seeing his opportunity, cut the cable or loosed the ship of [Quesada], so that it drifted upon that of Magellan, who came up, shouting: "Treason! treason!"

Upon which he entered the ship [the *San Antonio*] of [Quesada], and took him and his men prisoners, and [restored as] captain of the ship [the *San An-*

The Straits of Magellan today

tonio] one Alvaro de Mesquita, whom Cartagena had arrested and put in irons, because [Mesquita] found fault with him for the mutiny which he was making. Seeing this, the other ship [the *Concepción,* under Cartagena] at once surrendered.

He ordered Cartagena to be [marooned], having him publicly cried as a traitor; and the body of Luís de Mendoza . . . was quartered; and he ordered the quarters . . . to be set on shore, spitted on poles. [Quesada was beheaded.] So the Castilians had great fear of him, for he kept the mutineers prisoners in irons, and set to the pumps, during three months that he remained in this river, in which he [overhauled] and refitted his ships very well. When he was about to set sail, he ordered the prisoners to be set at liberty, and pardoned them.

"BIG FEET"

One day, about two months after the mutiny—June, 1520—Pigafetta and his comrades looked toward the wind-swept shore of St. Julian and saw something that might have come from a dream—or a nightmare. It was a giant Indian, who seemed to the short Mediterranean sailors to be about eight feet tall.

Magellan's men were friendly, and more giants appeared. They wore light brown skins of the guanaco, a small, camel-like llamá. Their faces were painted to keep the wind from chapping them, and their feet were bundled in guanaco boots which were stuffed with straw against the cold.

"Big Feet," Magellan named them—"Patagonians," in Spanish. The southern part of Argentina where they lived is still called Patagonia.

The Patagonians were nomads and expert hunters. They followed the guanaco, which provided their food and clothing, up and down their arid wasteland. These men were perhaps the fastest runners in the world, since with their Stone Age bows and arrows they had to overtake their game in order to kill it. Pigafetta's description of them as eight feet tall created a sensation in Europe. Actually the Patagonians were at most six feet four inches tall or a little more.

Pigafetta's narrative continues below.

We passed two months in that place [St. Julian] without seeing anyone. One day we suddenly saw a naked man of giant stature on the shore of the port, dancing, singing, and throwing dust on his head. The captain-general sent one of our men to the giant so that he might perform the same actions as a sign of peace. Having done that, the man led the giant to an islet into the presence of the captain-general. When the giant was in the captain-general's and our presence, he marvelled greatly, and made signs with one finger raised upward, believing that we had come from the sky.

He was so tall that we reached only to his waist, and he was well proportioned. His face was large and painted red all over, while about his eyes he was painted yellow; and he had two hearts painted on the middle of his cheeks. His scanty hair was painted white. He was dressed in the skins of animals skillfully sewn together. That animal has a head and ears as large as those of a mule, a neck and body like those of a camel, the legs of a deer, and the tail of a horse, like which it neighs, and that land has very many of them.

His feet were shod with the same kind of skins which covered his feet in the manner of shoes. In his hand he carried a short, heavy bow, with a cord somewhat thicker than those of the lute, and made from the intestines of the same animal, and a bundle of rather short cane arrows feathered like ours, and with points of white and black flint stones in the manner of Turkish arrows, instead of iron. Those points were fashioned by means of another stone.

The captain-general had the giant given something to eat and drink, and among other things which were shown to him was a large steel mirror. When he saw his face, he was greatly terrified, and jumped back throwing three or four of our men to the ground. After that he was given some bells, a mirror, a comb, and certain Pater Nosters [rosaries]. The captain-general sent him ashore with four armed men.

When one of his companions, who would never come to the ships, saw him coming with our men, he ran to the place where the others were, who came down to the shore all naked one after the other. When our men reached them, they began to dance and to sing, lifting one finger to the sky. They showed our men some white powder made from the roots of an herb, which they kept in earthen pots, and which they ate because they had nothing else. Our men made signs inviting them to the ships, [saying] that they would help them carry their possessions. Thereupon, those men quickly took only their bows, while their women laden like asses carried everything.

The latter are not so tall as the men but are very much fatter. When we saw them we were greatly surprised. . . . They are painted and clothed like their husbands. . . . They led four of those young animals [guanacos], fastened with thongs like a halter.

When those people wish to catch some of those animals, they tie one of these young ones to a thorn-bush. Thereupon, the large ones come to play with the little ones; and those people kill them with their arrows from their place of concealment. Our men led eighteen of those people, counting men and women, to the ships, and they were distributed on the two sides of the port so that they might catch some of the said animals.

JOHN THE GIANT

An especially cheerful Patagonian visited the fleet a few days later and stayed so long that the sailors had him baptized. They named him *Juan Gigante*—(John the Giant).

Six days after the above [June, 1520], a giant painted and clothed in the same manner was seen by some of our men who were cutting wood. He had a bow and arrows in his hand. When our men approached him, he first touched his head, face, and body, and then did the same to our men, afterward lifting his hands toward the sky. When the captain-general was informed of it, he ordered him to be brought in the small boat. He was taken to that island in the port where our men had built a house for the smiths and for the storage of some things from the ships.

That man was even taller and better built than the others and as tractable and amiable. Jumping up and down, he danced, and when he danced, at every leap, his feet sank . . . into the earth.

He remained with us for a considerable number of days, so long that we baptized him, calling him John. He uttered the words *Jesu, Pater Noster, Ave Maria* . . . as distinctly as we, but with an exceedingly loud voice. Then the captain-general gave him a shirt, a woollen jerkin, cloth breeches, a cap, a mirror, a comb, bells, and other things, and sent him away like his companions. He left us very joyous and happy.

The following day he brought one of those large animals [a guanaco] to the captain-general, in return for which many things were given to him, so that he might bring some more to us; but we did not see him again. We thought that his companions had killed him because he had conversed with us.

CAPTIVES AND CUSTOMS

Magellan played a cruel trick—Pigafetta calls it a "cunning trick"—to capture two Patagonians whom he planned to take back to Spain. Explorers of the sixteenth century looked upon the Indians as scarcely human; they often thought of them as "specimens" to be brought back to rulers in Europe.

A fortnight later we saw four of those giants without their arms for they had hidden them in certain bushes as the two whom we captured showed us. Each one was painted differently. The captain-general kept two of them—the youngest and best proportioned—by means of a very cunning trick, in order to take them to Spain. Had he used any other means than those he employed, they could easily have killed some of us.

The trick that he employed in keeping them was as follows. He gave them many knives, scissors, mirrors, bells, and glass beads; and those two having their hands filled with the said articles, the captain-general had two pairs of iron manacles brought, such as are fastened on the feet. He made motions that he would give them to the giants, whereat they were very pleased, since those manacles were of iron, but they did not know how to carry them. They were grieved at leaving them behind, but they had no place to put those gifts; for they had to hold the skin wrapped about them with their hands. The other two giants wished to help them, but the captain refused.

Seeing that they were loath to leave these manacles behind, the captain made them a sign that he would put them on their feet, and that they could carry them away. They nodded assent with the head. Immediately, the captain had the manacles put on both of them at the same time. When our men were driving home the cross bolt, the giants began to suspect something, but the captain assuring them, however, they stood still.

When they saw later that they were tricked, they raged like bulls, calling loudly for *Setebos* to aid them. With difficulty could we bind the hands of the other two, whom we sent ashore with nine of our men, in order that the giants might guide them to the place where the wife of one of the two whom we had captured was; for the latter expressed his great grief at leaving her by signs so that we understood that he meant her.

While they were on their way, one of the giants freed his hands, and took to his heels with such swiftness that our men lost sight of him. He went to the place where his associates were, but he did not find there one of his companions, who had remained behind with the women, and who had gone hunting. He immediately went in search of the latter, and told him all that had happened.

The other giant endeavoured so hard to free himself from his bonds, that our men struck him, wounding him slightly on the head, whereat he raging led them to where the women were. Juan Carvalho, the pilot and commander of those men, refused to bring back the woman that night, but determined to sleep there, for night was approaching. The other two giants came, and seeing their companion wounded, hesitated, but said nothing then. But with the dawn, they spoke to the women, whereupon they immediately ran away (and the smaller ones ran faster than the taller), leaving all their possessions behind them.

Two of them turned aside to shoot their arrows at our men. The other was leading away those small animals of theirs in order to hunt. Thus fighting, one of them pierced the thigh of one of our men with an arrow, and the latter died immediately.

When the giants saw that, they ran away quickly. Our men had muskets and crossbows, but they could never hit any of the giants, for when the latter fought, they never stood still, but leaped hither and thither. Our men buried their dead companion, and burned all the possessions left behind by the giants. Of a truth those giants run swifter than horses and are exceedingly jealous of their wives. . . .

They wear their hair cut with the tonsure, like friars, but it is left longer; and they have a cotton cord wrapped about the head, to which they fasten their arrows when they go hunting. . . .

When one of those people dies, ten or twelve demons all painted appear to them and dance very joyfully about the corpse. They notice that one of those demons is much taller than the others, and he cries out and rejoices more. They paint themselves exactly in the same manner as the demon appears to them painted.

They call the larger demon *Setebos,* and the others *Cheleulle*. That giant also told us by signs that he had seen the demons with two horns on their heads, and long hair which hung to the feet, belching forth fire.

Shakespeare, who read parts of Pigafetta's narrative in Richard Eden's *Decades of the New World* (1555), put Setebos in one of his plays. In *The Tempest* Setebos is the god worshipped by a character named Caliban. Caliban, an uncouth "freckl'd whelp," may himself have been drawn, in part, from Pigafetta's descriptions of the Patagonian giants.

WRECK OF THE *SANTIAGO*

While still in winter quarters Magellan repaired his ships—and made a startling discovery. He worked on his vessels by "careening" them. That is, he floated a ship up on the beach at high tide, anchored it, then "careened," or tilted it to one side by shifting all the cannon over to that side. As the tide ebbed, the crew propped timbers under the hull and placed scaffolding on the upper or high side. Then they climbed up the scaffolding to scrape away barnacles, replace worn planks, and recaulk the seams. At the next high tide the ship was tilted in the opposite direction and its other side cleaned.

In order to careen the ships Magellan unloaded the cargo, stored it in temporary sheds, and made his unhappy discovery. He found he had exactly one half as much wine and biscuit as he was supposed to have. The clever Portuguese consul, Alvarez, in Seville had bribed officials to give Magellan two receipts for every one consignment of food. In six months the fleet would face starvation.

Magellan was terribly upset but told no one what he had learned. Instead he had a large amount of fish and seafowl smoked, salted, and packed in barrels, and he revised his exploring schedule. He sent the light *Santiago* out immediately on a scouting trip south to try to find the strait so the fleet could go on to the Spice Islands without spending the long winter at St. Julian.

Captain Juan Serrano, in command of the *Santiago*, had the worst of luck. After battling head winds for over two weeks, making only four miles a day, he came to a wide river which he named the Santa Cruz. Here he was just two days' sail from the strait when, on May 22, 1520, an easterly gale smashed his rudder and hurled the *Santiago* on a spit of sand, where it broke up. The crew escaped and two volunteers, as described below, struggled back to St. Julian with the news.

A ship called *Santiago* was wrecked in an expedition made to explore the coast. All the men were saved as by a miracle, not even getting wet. Two of them came to the ships after suffering great hardships, and reported the whole occurrence to us. Consequently, the captain-general sent some men with bags full of biscuits sufficient to last for two months.

It was necessary for us to carry them the food, for daily pieces of the ship that was wrecked were found. The way thither was long, being twenty-four leagues . . . and the path was very rough and full of thorns. The men were four days on the road, sleeping at night in the bushes. They found no drinking water, but only ice, which caused them the greatest hardship.

There were very many long shellfish which are called *missiglioni* in that port of St. Julian. They have pearls, although small ones in the middle, but could not be eaten. Incense, ostriches, foxes, sparrows, and rabbits much smaller than ours were also found. We erected a cross on the top of the highest summit there, as a sign in that land that it belonged to the king of Spain; and we called that summit Monte de Christo.

CHAPTER FOUR

THE STRAIT OF MAGELLAN

August 24, 1520 — March 16, 1521

On the 21st of the said month [October, 1520], I took the [altitude of the] sun in exactly 52° [south latitude], at five leagues from the land, and there we saw an opening like a bay, and it has at the entrance, on the right hand a very long spit of sand, and the cape which we discovered before this spit, is called the Cape of the Virgins . . . and within this bay we found a strait. . . . In this strait there are a great many elbows, and the chains of mountains are very high and covered with snow, with much forest.

—The Log-Book of Francisco Albo

DISCOVERY IN A STORM

After the loss of the *Santiago* and the rescue of the survivors, Magellan decided to exchange his winter quarters at ill-fated St. Julian for new ones farther south. On August 24, 1520, he sailed to Rio Santa Cruz (the "river of fresh water" mentioned below), where he encamped for another two months. Cartagena and a traitorous priest were marooned at St. Julian.

Now the jealous chief pilot, Gomes, stirred up the officers to urge Magellan to abandon his search for a strait and go east to the Spice Islands by way of the Cape of Good Hope. Magellan refused; he would sail right into the Antarctic Circle—as far as 75° south latitude—before admitting defeat. On October 18, 1520, the fleet left Rio Santa Cruz and headed south into a howling polar storm.

Pigafetta's narrative continues below.

Leaving [St. Julian], we found, in fifty-one degrees less one-third degree, toward the Antarctic Pole, a river of fresh water. There the ships almost perished because of the furious winds; but God and the holy bodies aided them.

We stayed about two months [September and October, 1520] in that river [Santa Cruz] in order to supply the ships with water, wood, and fish, the latter being half a yard in length and more, and covered with scales. They were very good although small. Before leaving that river, the captain-general and all of us confessed and received communion as true Christians.

Then going to fifty-two degrees toward the same pole, we found a strait on the day of the Feast of the

Eleven Thousand Virgins [October 21, 1520], whose head [we] called Cape of the Eleven Thousand Virgins because of that very great miracle. That strait . . . is surrounded by very lofty mountains laden with snow. There it was impossible to find bottom for anchoring, [and] it was necessary to fasten the moorings on land twelve or fifteen yards away.

Had it not been for the captain-general, we would not have found that strait, for we all thought and said that it was closed on all sides. But the captain-general who knew where to sail to find a well-hidden strait, which he saw depicted on a map in the treasury of the king of Portugal, which was made by that excellent man, Martin Behaim, sent two ships, the *San Antonio*

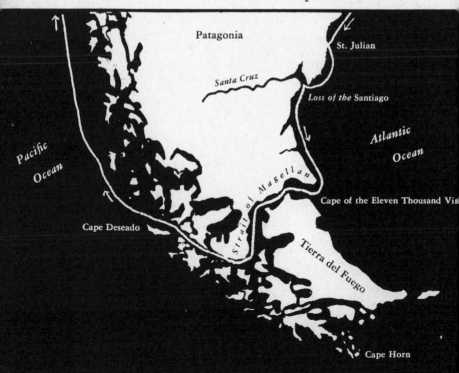

and the *Concepción* . . . to discover what was inside the cape of the bay. We with the other two ships, the flagship, called *Trinidad*, and the other the *Victoria*, stayed inside the bay to await them.

A great storm struck us that night, which lasted until the middle of next day, which necessitated our lifting anchor, and letting ourselves drift hither and thither about the bay. The other two ships suffered a headwind and could not double a cape formed by the bay almost at its end, as they were trying to return to join us; so that they thought that they would have to run aground.

But on approaching the end of the bay, and thinking that they were lost, they saw a small opening which did not appear to be an opening, but a sharp turn. Like desperate men they hauled into it, and thus they discovered the strait by chance. Seeing that it was not a sharp turn, but a strait with land, they proceeded farther, and found a bay. And then farther on they found another strait and another bay larger than the first two. Very joyful they immediately turned back to inform the captain-general.

We thought that they had been wrecked, first, by reason of the violent storm, and second, because two days had passed and they had not appeared, and also because of certain signals with smoke made by two of their men who had been sent ashore to advise us.

And so, while in suspense, we saw the two ships with sails full and banners flying to the wind, coming toward us. When they neared us in this manner, they suddenly discharged a number of mortars, and burst into cheers. Then all together thanking God and the Virgin Mary, we went to seek the strait farther on.

Pigafetta's saying that Magellan saw his strait "depicted on a map in the treasury of the king of Portugal, which was made by that excellent man, Martin Behaim" is one reason for believing that Magellan was influenced in his theories about a strait by Behaim's globe (see page 10). Magellan examined maps, globes, etc. in the royal chartroom in Lisbon before he left for Spain (see p. xxxii).

THE *SAN ANTONIO* RUNS AWAY

After entering that strait, we found two openings, one to the south-east, and the other to the south-west. The captain-general sent the ship *San Antonio* together with the *Concepción* to ascertain whether that opening which was toward the southeast had an exit into the [South Sea]. The ship *San Antonio* would not await the *Concepción*, because it intended to flee and return to Spain—which it did.

The pilot of [the *San Antonio*] was one Estevan Gomes, and he hated the captain-general exceedingly, because before that fleet was fitted out, the emperor had ordered that he be given some caravels with which to discover lands, but his Majesty did not give them to him because of the coming of the captain-general. On that account he conspired with certain Spaniards, and next night they captured the captain of their ship, a cousin of the captain-general, one Alvaro de Mesquita, whom they wounded and put in irons, and in this condition took to Spain. The other giant whom we had captured was in that ship, but he died when the heat came on. The *Concepción*, as it could not follow that ship, waited for it, sailing about hither and thither. The *San Antonio* turned back at night and fled along the same strait.

We [on the *Trinidad* and *Victoria*] had gone to explore the other opening toward the southwest. Finding, however, the same strait continuously, we came upon a river which we called the river of Sardine. . . . So we stayed there for four days in order to await the [other] two ships.

During that period [early November, 1520] we sent a well-equipped boat to explore the cape of the other sea. The men returned within three days, and reported that they had seen the cape and the open sea. The captain-general wept for joy, and called that cape, Cape Deseado [Desired], for we had been desiring it for a long time.

We turned back to look for the [other] two ships, but we found only the *Concepción*. Upon asking them where the other one was [the *San Antonio*], Juan Serrano, who was captain and pilot of the [*Concepción*] . . . replied that he did not know, and that he had never seen it after it had entered the opening. We sought it in all parts of the strait, as far as that opening whence it had fled, and the captain-general sent the ship *Victoria* back to the entrance of the strait to ascertain whether the ship was there.

Orders were given them, if they did not find it, to plant a banner on the summit of some small hill with a letter in an earthen pot buried in the earth near the banner, so that if the banner were seen the letter might be found, and the ship might learn the course that we were sailing. For this was the arrangement made between us in case that we went astray one from the other.

Two banners were planted with their letters—one on a little eminence in the first bay, and the other in an islet in the third bay where there were many sea-wolves and large birds. The captain-general waited for [the *Victoria*] . . . near the river of Isleo, and he had a cross set up in an islet near that river, which flowed between high mountains covered with snow and emptied into the sea near the river of Sardine.

Had we not discovered that strait, the captain-general had determined to go as far as seventy-five degrees toward the Antarctic Pole.

The desertion of the *San Antonio* was a heavy blow to Magellan. It was his largest ship (120 tons), carrying over sixty men and a good share of his supplies—especially food. Six months later the runaway ship arrived in Seville, where Gomes puzzled the officials by his bitter accusations against Magellan. Much later, when Magellan's men finally returned from their trip around the world in the *Victoria*, the officials threw Gomes in jail.

Meanwhile the bewildered Magellan consulted the fleet's

astrologer. This gentleman cast his horoscope and announced that there had been a mutiny on the *San Antonio* and that the ship had gone back to Spain. Anticipating that charges would be made against him, Magellan then issued an order of the day, calling for written statements of opinion from his officers as to whether or not to proceed with the voyage.

MAGELLAN'S ORDER OF THE DAY

November 21, 1520

I, Ferdinand Magellan, Knight of the Order of St. James, and captain-general of this fleet, which his majesty sent for the discovery of the spices, etc.

I make known to you, Duarte Barbosa, captain of the ship *Victoria*, and to the pilots, masters, and quartermasters of that ship, as I have understood that it seems to you all a serious matter, that I am determined to go forward, because it seems to you that the weather is little fitted for this voyage on which we are going;

and inasmuch as I am a man who never rejected the opinion or counsel of any one, but rather all my affairs are discussed and communicated generally to all, without any person being affronted by me; and since, because of that which happened in the port of St. Julian with respect to the death of Luís de Mendoza, Gaspar de Quesada, and the banishment of Juan de Cartagena and Pero Sanchez de Reina, the priest, you, from fear, desist from telling me, and counselling all that may appear to you to be for the service of his majesty, and the safe conduct of this fleet, and you have not told it me nor counselled it:

you err in the service of the emperor and king our sovereign, and go against the oath and plighted homage which you have made to me; for which I command you on the part of the said sovereign, and on my part beseech you and charge you, that with respect to all that you think is fitting for our voyage, both as to going forward, and as to turning back, that you give me your opinions in writing each one for himself: declaring the circumstances and reasons why we ought to go forward or turn back, not having respect to anything for which you should omit to tell the truth.

With which reasons and opinions, I will say mine, and my decision for coming to a conclusion as to what we have to do.

Done in the Channel of All Saints, opposite the river of the islet [Isleo], on Wednesday, November 21, in fifty-three degrees, of the year 1520.

The only response to Magellan's order which survives is that of the fleet astrologer, Andrés de San Martín. It is a very negative document, but probably the other officers agreed with San Martín. The astrologer was (1) against voyaging any farther south—it was too cold; (2) against sailing at night, as Magellan did—it was too tiring; (3) against going to the Spice Islands by way of the Cape of Good Hope—it was too far. He asserted that the strait did not lead to the Moluccas and suggested another two months' exploration, then a speedy return home.

Actually Magellan wanted his officers' opinions only for

the record; his own mind was made up. Just after the discovery of the strait, at a council of officers he had declared: "Even if we have to eat the leather wrappings on the masts and yards, I will still go on to discover what I have promised Our Lord the King, and I trust that God will aid us and give us good fortune." He now (November 23, 1520) reaffirmed this decision, swearing by the habit of the Knights of Santiago, which he wore, to continue the voyage into the Great South Sea.

LAND OF FIRE

The first published account of Magellan's voyage, by Maximilian of Transylvania, secretary of Charles V, describes some fires not mentioned by Pigafetta. From these fires along the south shore of the strait the land at the tip of South America received its name: Tierra del Fuego (Land of Fire).

The month of November was upon them, the night was rather more than five hours long, and they had never seen any human beings on the shore.

But one night a great number of fires were seen, mostly on their left hand, from which they guessed that they had been seen by the natives of the region. But Magellan, seeing that the country was rocky, and also stark with eternal cold, thought it useless to waste many days in examining it; and so, with only three ships, he continued on his course along the channel. . . .

There is no doubt that the land which they had upon their right was the continent of which we have spoken, but they think that the land on the left was

An artist's impression of the discovery of the Straits of Magellan

not a mainland, but islands, because sometimes on that side they heard on a still farther coast the beating and roaring of the sea.

Tierra del Fuego is at the southernmost tip of South America. The fires were built on mounds of earth in hollow log canoes and kept perpetually burning because the Stone Age natives, even more primitive than the Patagonians, did not know how to make a new fire.

FLYING FISH

Magellan brought his remaining three ships, the *Trinidad*, *Concepción*, and *Victoria*, safely through the strait—a voyage of 360 miles, lasting over a month. However, after the desertion of the *San Antonio* he had fewer than two hundred men left.

The captain-general called the strait the Channel of All Saints. Other names suggested for it were the Strait of Victoria (after the ship which first sighted it), the Strait of the Mother of God, and the Strait of Martin Behaim. Pigafetta called it the Strait of Patagonia. But from the first it also bore the name by which it will always be known: the Strait of Magellan.

Pigafetta's narrative continues below.

We called that strait the strait of Patagonia. One finds the safest of ports every half league in it, water, the finest of wood (but not of cedar), fish, sardines, and [shellfish], while smallage, a sweet herb (although there is also some that is bitter) grows around the springs. We ate of it for many days as we had nothing else. I believe that there is not a more beautiful or better strait in the world than that one.

In that Ocean Sea one sees a very amusing fish hunt. The fish that hunt are of three sorts, and are half a yard and more in length, and are called *dorado, albicore,* and *bonito.* Those fish follow the flying fish . . . which are one palm and more in length and very good to eat.

When the above three kinds of fish find any of those flying fish, the latter immediately leap from the water and fly as long as their wings are wet—more than a crossbow's flight. While they are flying, the others run along behind them under the water following the shadow of the flying fish. The latter have no sooner fallen into the water than the others immediately seize and eat them. It is in fine a very amusing thing to watch.

WORDS OF THE PATAGONIANS

Pigafetta introduces here a long list of Patagonian words, the first list ever compiled, from which the examples below are taken. The Patagonian language is said to have changed little since Magellan's time.

Words of the Patagonian giants:

for Head	her
for Eye	other
for Hand	chene
for to Scratch	gechare
for Cross-eyed man	calischen

for Fire	ghialeme
for No	ehen
for Yes	rey
for Sun	calexcheni
for Stars	settere
for Wind	oni
for Fish	hoi
for Snow	theu
for Ostrich, a bird	hoihoi
for Parrot	cheche
for their big Devil	Setebos
for their small Devils	Cheleulle

All the above words are pronounced in the throat, for such is their method of pronunciation.

That giant whom we had in our ship told me those words; for when he, upon asking me for *capac,* that is to say, bread, as they call that root which they use as bread, and *oli,* that is to say, water, saw me write those words quickly, and afterward when I, with pen in hand, asked him for other words, he understood me.

Once I made the sign of the cross, and, showing it to him, kissed it. He immediately cried out, "Setebos," and made me a sign that if I made the sign of the cross again, Setebos would enter into my body and cause it to burst. [Later] when that giant was sick, he asked for the cross, and embracing it and kissing it many times, desired to become a Christian before his death. We called him Paul.

When those people wish to make a fire, they rub a sharpened piece of wood against another piece until the fire catches in the pith of a certain tree, which is placed between those two sticks.

STARVATION AT SEA

As Magellan's little fleet, consisting now of the *Trinidad*, *Concepción*, and *Victoria*, entered the unknown ocean on November 28, 1520, the captain-general had the priest bless the ships. The crews chanted a *Te Deum* and fired their cannon.

"Gentlemen," Magellan addressed his officers on the quarterdeck of the *Trinidad*, "we now are steering into waters where no ship has sailed before. May we always find them as peaceful as they are this morning. In this hope I shall name this sea the *Mar Pacifico*." Thus the Pacific received its name.

But Magellan's earlier words, "Even if we have to eat the leather wrappings on the masts and yards, I will still go on," proved prophetic. If he had started diagonally across the Pacific sooner, instead of heading up the coast of Chile to escape the cold, he would have encountered a chain of islands providing food and water most of the way.

As it was, his fleet sailed two months without sighting land, three months without the badly needed fresh fruit and vegetables. (Columbus was at sea only a month in his discovery of America.) Scurvy, caused by poor diet, took a terrible toll of Magellan's crews.

Wednesday, November 28, 1520, we debouched from that strait, engulfing ourselves in the Pacific Sea. We were three months and twenty days without getting any kind of fresh food. We ate biscuit, which was no longer biscuit, but powder of biscuits swarming with worms, for they had eaten the good. It stank strongly . . . of rats. We drank yellow water that had been putrid for many days.

We also ate some ox hides that covered the top of the mainyard to prevent the yard from chafing the shrouds, and which had become exceedingly hard because of the sun, rain, and wind. We left them in the sea for four or five days, and then placed them for a few moments on top of the embers, and so ate them; and often we ate sawdust from boards. Rats were sold for one-half ducat apiece, and even we could not get them.

But above all the other misfortunes the following was the worst. The gums of both the lower and upper teeth of some of our men swelled, so that they could not eat under any circumstances and therefore died. Nineteen men died from that sickness [scurvy], and the giant together with an Indian from the country of Brazil. Twenty-five or thirty men fell sick during that time, in the arms, legs, or in another place, so that but few remained well. However, I by the grace of God, suffered no sickness.

We sailed about four thousand leagues during those three months and twenty days through an open stretch in that Pacific Sea. In truth it is very pacific, for during that time we did not suffer any storm. We saw no land except two desert islets, where we found nothing but birds and trees, for which we called them the Unfortunate Isles. They are two hundred leagues apart. We found no anchorage, but near them saw many sharks. The first islet lies in fifteen degrees of south latitude, and the other in nine.

Daily we made runs of fifty, sixty, or seventy leagues. . . . Had not God and His blessed mother given us so good weather we would all have died of hunger in that exceeding vast sea. Of a verity I believe no such voyage will ever be made again.

When we left that strait, if we had sailed continuously westward we would have circumnavigated the world without finding other land than the Cape of the Eleven Thousand Virgins.

UNDER THE SOUTHERN CROSS

Below Pigafetta describes some of the stars seen and also the course Magellan followed. The "many small stars clustered together" have been named "the Magellanic clouds." They are distant galaxies.

The course followed was roughly northwest until the fleet crossed the equator, at about 165° west longitude, and reached a point nine hundred miles north of it. Then Magellan turned and headed due west, toward the Philippine Islands (13° north latitude). Yet he knew that the Moluccas were along the equator.

To increase the mystery, Pigafetta says that their goal was "Cape Cattigara," supposed to be the southernmost point of the mainland of Asia.

Apparently Magellan was seeking some other land first. One theory is that he planned to go to the Philippines, which he may have visited during his previous service in the

East, and claim them for Spain. Another theory is that he was looking for a country of fabulous wealth, the Biblical Tarshish and Ophir, supposed to be near Cattigara. These lands have recently been identified as Formosa and the Ryukyu Islands off the coast of China. Magellan did not sail far enough north to hit them, however.

In Magellan's day 0° longitude did not pass through Greenwich, England, as now, but through the Canary Islands. Distances east and west around the world were measured, very inaccurately, from this meridian. Because of the difficulty of determining longitude, navigators usually practised "parallel sailing." That is, they sailed to the latitude on which their destination lay, then went east or west along that latitude to their destination.

The Antarctic Pole is not so starry as the Arctic. Many small stars clustered together are seen, which have the appearance of two clouds of mist [the Magellanic clouds]. There is but little distance between them, and they are somewhat dim. In the midst of them are two large and not very luminous stars, which move only slightly. Those two stars are the Antarctic Pole.

Our [compass needle], although it moved hither and thither, always pointed toward its own Arctic Pole, although it did not have so much strength as on its own side. And on that account when we were in that open expanse, the captain-general, asking all the pilots whether they were always sailing forward in the course which we had laid down on the maps, all replied: "By your course exactly as laid down." He an-

swered them that they were pointing wrongly—
which was a fact—and that it would be fitting to
adjust the needle of navigation. . . .

The paragraph above refers to the "variation of the
compass," the fact that in different parts of the world the
compass needle falls off a little to one side or the other instead of pointing due north. On Magellan's crossing the
variation was to the north-west. Columbus, Magellan, and
other explorers were among the first to observe this phe-
nomenon.

When we were in the midst of that open expanse,
we saw a cross [the Southern Cross] with five extremely bright stars straight toward the west, those
stars being exactly placed with regard to one another.
During those days we sailed west north-west, north-
west by west, and north-west, until we reached the
equinoctial line [the equator]. . . . After we had
passed the equinoctial line we sailed west north-west,
and west by north, and then for two hundred leagues
toward the west, changing our course to west by
south until we reached thirteen degrees toward the
Arctic Pole in order that we might approach nearer
to the land of Cape Cattigara.

ISLANDS OF THIEVES

Magellan's first landfall, not counting the disappointing
"desert islets" where there were no provisions, was Guam,
a famous battleground in World War II. Guam is one of
the Mariana Islands, located fifteen hundred miles east
of the Philippines.

E

Magellan's men wept and intoned the *Laudate Domine* when they at last sighted land. Later they called these islands *Islas de los Ladrones*, "Islands of Thieves." The natives swarmed around the fleet in their swift outrigger canoes, curious and also contemptuous of the feeble crews. Because of the weakness of his men from scurvy and starvation, Magellan's expedition was in great danger here.

About seventy leagues on the above course, and lying in twelve degrees of [north] latitude . . . we discovered on Wednesday, March 6, [1521], a small island to the north-west, and two others toward the south-west, one of which was higher and larger than the other two.

The captain-general wished to stop at the large island and get some fresh food, but he was unable to do so because the inhabitants of that island entered the ships and stole whatever they could lay their hands on, so that we could not protect ourselves. The men were about to strike the sails so that we could go ashore, but the natives very deftly stole from us the small boat that was fastened to the poop of the flagship.

Thereupon, the captain-general in wrath went ashore with forty armed men, who burned some forty or fifty houses together with many boats, and killed seven men. He recovered the small boat, and we departed immediately pursuing the same course. Before we landed, some of our sick men begged us if we should kill any man or woman to bring the entrails to them, as they would recover immediately.

When we wounded any of those people with our crossbowshafts, which passed completely through their loins from one side to the other, they, looking at it, pulled on the shaft now on this and now on that side, and then drew it out, with great astonishment, and so died. Others who were wounded in the breast did the same, which moved us to great compassion.

Those people seeing us departing followed us with more than one hundred boats for more than one league. They approached the ships showing us fish, feigning that they would give them to us; but then threw stones at us and fled. And although the ships were under full sail [March 9, 1521], they passed between them and the small boats fastened astern, very adroitly in those small boats of theirs. We saw some women in their boats who were crying out and tearing their hair, for love, I believe, of those whom we had killed.

Each one of those people lives according to his own will, for they have no seignior. They go naked, and some are bearded and have black hair that reaches to the waist. They wear small palm-leaf hats, as do the Albanians. They are as tall as we, and well built. They have no worship. They are tawny, but are born white. Their teeth are red and black, for they think that is most beautiful.

The women go naked except that they wear a narrow strip of bark as thin as paper. . . . They are good-looking and delicately formed, and lighter complexioned than the men; and wear their hair which is exceedingly black, loose and hanging quite down to the ground. The women do not work in the fields but stay in the house, weaving mats, baskets, and other things needed in their houses, from palm leaves.

They eat coconuts, camotes [sweet potatoes], birds, figs one palm in length [bananas], sugar cane, and flying fish, besides other things. They anoint the body and the hair with coconut and beniseed oil. Their houses are all built of wood covered with planks and thatched with leaves of the fig tree [banana tree] a yard long; and they have floors and windows. The rooms and the beds are all furnished with the most beautiful palm-leaf mats. They sleep on palm straw which is very soft and fine.

They use no weapons, except a kind of a spear pointed with a fishbone at the end. Those people are poor, but ingenious and very thievish, on account of which we called those three islands the Islands of Thieves.

Their amusement, men and women, is to plough the seas with those small boats of theirs. Those boats resemble *fucelere* [small, swift Venetian vessels], but are narrower, and some are black, some white, and others red. At the side opposite the sail, they have a large piece of wood pointed at the top, with poles laid across it and resting on the water, in order that the boats may sail more safely. The sail is made from palm leaves sewn together and is shaped like a lateen sail. For rudders they use a certain blade resembling a hearth shovel which have a piece of wood at the end. They can change stern and bow at will, and those boats resemble the dolphins which leap in the water from wave to wave.

Those [people] thought, according to the signs which they made, that there were no other people in the world but themselves.

CHAPTER FIVE

THE CROSS IN THE PHILIPPINES

March 16, 1521 — April 14, 1521

From the mouth of the channel of Cebu and Mactan we went west in mid-channel, and met with the town of Cebu, at which we anchored, and made peace, and there they gave us rice and millet and flesh; and we remained there many days; and the king and the queen, with many people, became Christians of their free will.

—*The Log-Book of Francisco Albo*

PALMS AND COCONUTS

Once upon a time a good-natured giant carried on his shoulders a country inhabited by men. The men had forests to hunt in, coconut groves and rice fields to cultivate, and comfortable bamboo houses to live in. But they were always quarrelling, never happy and never grateful. So one day the giant became indignant and flung their land into the sea. It broke into seven thousand fragments. These, according to the legend related to Magellan by a native chief, are the Philippine Islands.

After leaving Guam, Magellan sailed to this majestic archipelago stretching a thousand miles north and south off the coast of Asia. He named it St. Lazarus. Later the Spaniards, who claimed the Philippines as their farthest west possession, called them the Western Islands. The Portuguese, to support their claim to lands to the east, referred to them as the Eastern Islands. In 1542 the name Philippines was given to honour the son (Philip II) of Magellan's good friend Charles V.

Magellan discovered the Philippine Islands in 1521—or, possibly in 1512 when he made a mysterious exploratory voyage from Malacca. (He journeyed hundreds of miles east of Malacca, but historians are not certain what lands he reached.) When he sighted the headland of Samar in the pale morning light of March 16, 1521, he also became the first man to circumnavigate the earth. In the past he had voyaged from somewhere near the Philippines eastward to India, Africa, and Portugal; now he had come by the western route across the Atlantic and South Pacific back to his starting point.

Magellan may have set his course for the Philippines because he thought them rich in gold. When a native king sent him a bar of gold, Magellan exclaimed, "I am now in the land I hoped to reach!" His first task, however, was to rest his men and heal those who had scurvy. He had tents placed on the shore of Leyte Gulf and visited the sick

E*

himself every day, bringing them oranges, coconut milk, and kind words.

Pigafetta's narrative continues below.

At dawn on Saturday, March 16, 1521, we came upon a high land at a distance of three hundred leagues from the Islands of Thieves—an island named Samar [in the Philippines]. The following day, the captain-general desired to land on another island which was uninhabited and lay to the right of the above mentioned island, in order to be more secure, and to get water and have some rest. He had two tents set up on the shore for the sick and had a sow killed for them.

On Monday afternoon, March 18, we saw a boat coming toward us with nine men in it. Therefore, the captain-general ordered that no one should move or say a word without his permission. When those men reached the shore, their chief went immediately to the captain-general, giving signs of joy because of our arrival. Five of the most ornately adorned of them remained with us, while the rest went to get some others who were fishing, and so they all came.

The captain-general seeing that they were reasonable men, ordered food to be set before them, and gave them red caps, mirrors, combs, bells, ivory . . . and other things. When they saw the captain's courtesy, they presented fish, a jar of palm wine,

Map of the Philippines and the Spice

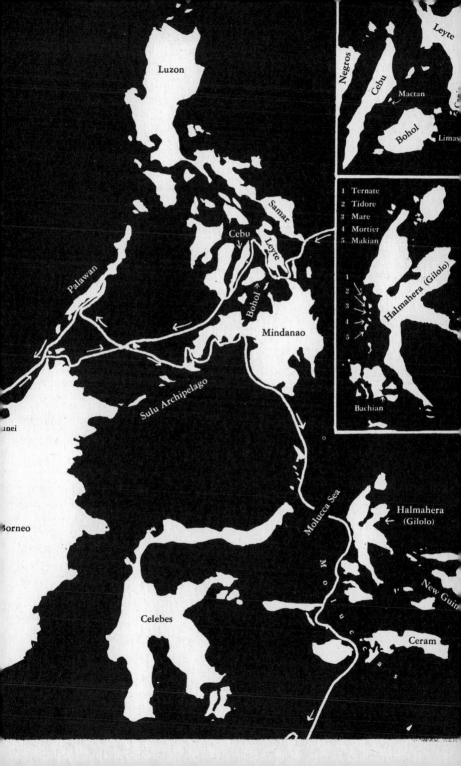

which they call *uraca*, figs [bananas] more than one palm long, and others which were smaller and more delicate, and two coconuts. They had nothing else then, but made us signs with their hands that they would bring *umay*, or rice, and coconuts and many other articles of food within four days.

Coconuts are the fruit of the palm tree. Just as we have bread, wine, oil, and milk, so those people get everything from that tree. They get wine in the following manner. They bore a hole into the heart of the said palm at the top . . . from which distills a liquor which resembles white must [new wine]. That liquor is sweet but somewhat tart, and is gathered in canes of bamboo as thick as the leg and thicker. They fasten the bamboo to the tree at evening for the morning, and in the morning for the evening.

That palm bears a fruit, namely, the coconut, which is as large as the head or thereabouts. Its outside husk is green and thicker than two fingers. Certain filaments are found in that husk, whence is made cord for binding together their boats. Under that husk there is a hard shell, much thicker than the shell of the walnut, which they burn and make therefrom a powder that is useful to them.

Under that shell there is a white marrowy substance one finger in thickness, which they eat fresh with meat and fish as we do bread; and it has a taste resembling the almond. It could be dried and made into bread. There is a clear, sweet water in the middle of

that marrowy substance which is very refreshing.
. . . A family of ten persons can be supported on two
trees, by utilizing them [alternately each week] for
the wine; for if they did otherwise, the trees would
dry up. They last a century. . . .

The island where we were is called Homonhon; but
inasmuch as we found two springs there of the clearest
water, we called it "the Watering-place of Good
Signs," for there were the first signs of gold which we
found in those districts. . . . There are many islands
in that district, and therefore we called them the archipelago of St. Lazarus, as they were discovered on
the Sabbath of St. Lazarus. They lie in ten degrees of
latitude toward the Arctic Pole, and in a longitude
of one hundred and sixty-one degrees from the line of
demarcation. . . .

We stayed there one week, and during that time
our captain went ashore daily to visit the sick, and
every morning gave them coconut water from his
own hand, which comforted them greatly. There are
people living near that island who have holes in their
ears so large that they can pass their arms through
them. Those people are *caphri*, that is to say, heathen.
They go naked [but for] a cloth woven from the
bark of a tree . . . except some of the chiefs who
wear cotton cloth embroidered with silk at the ends
by means of a needle.

They are dark, fat, and painted. They anoint themselves with coconut and with beniseed oil, as a protec-

tion against sun and wind. They have very black hair that falls to the waist, and use daggers, knives, and spears ornamented with gold, large shields, fascines [darts], javelins, and fishing nets . . . and their boats are like ours.

THE KING SPEAKS MALAY

Pigafetta now narrates one of the dramatic moments of Magellan's voyage—the first encounter with natives who understood Malay. Malay is the common language of the East Indies. When Rajah Colambu's men answered Magellan's slave (Enrique de Malacca) in his own language, Magellan knew that his great goal had been attained. He had indeed reached the East by sailing west.

Further proof that he was in the Orient came to Magellan from the natives' white porcelain jars with coloured flower designs. Magellan recognized the jars as a type originating in Canton, China. And he was undoubtedly familiar, from previous years in the Orient, with the Malay ceremony of *casi casi* in which each of two men tasted a little of the other's blood and swore brotherhood.

The brown-skinned natives were of Malay stock. Magellan found them good navigators, very courteous, rather lazy and pleasure-loving, and loyal to their rajahs.

On Thursday morning, March 28, [1521], as we had seen a fire on an island [named Limasaua] the night before, we anchored near it. We saw a small boat which the natives call *boloto* with eight men in it, approaching the flagship. A slave belonging to the

captain-general, who was a native of Sumatra . . .
spoke to them.

They immediately understood him, came alongside
the ship, unwilling to enter but taking a position at
some little distance. The captain seeing that they
would not trust us, threw them out a red cap and
other things tied to a bit of wood. They received
them very gladly, and went away quickly to advise
their king.

About two hours later we saw two *balanghai* coming. They are large boats and are so called by those
people. They were full of men, and their king was in
the larger of them, being seated under an awning of
mats. When the king came near the flagship, the slave
spoke to him. The king understood him. . . . He
ordered some of his men to enter the ships, but he
always remained in his *balanghai*, at some little distance from the ship, until his own men returned; and
as soon as they returned he departed.

The captain-general showed great honour to the men
who entered the ship, and gave them some presents,
for which the king wished before his departure to give
the captain a large bar of gold and a basketful of
ginger. The latter, however, thanked the king heartily
but would not accept it. In the afternoon we went in
the ships and anchored near the dwellings of the king.

Next day, [Good] Friday, the captain-general sent
his slave, who acted as our interpreter, ashore in a
small boat to ask the king [Rajah Colambu, of Li-

masaua] if he had any food to have it carried to the ships; and to say that they would be well satisfied with us, for he and his men had come to the island as friends and not as enemies.

The king came with six or eight men in the same boat and entered the ship. He embraced the captain-general to whom he gave three porcelain jars covered with leaves and full of raw rice, two very large fish, and other things. The captain-general gave the king a garment of red and yellow cloth made in the Turkish fashion, and a fine red cap; and to the others (the king's men) . . . knives and . . . mirrors. Then the captain-general had a collation spread for them, and had the king told through the slave that he desired to be *casi casi* with him, that is to say, [to be his] brother. The king replied that he also wished to enter the same relations with the captain-general.

Then the captain showed him cloth of various colours, linen, coral ornaments, and many other articles of merchandise, and all the artillery, some of which he had discharged for him, whereat the natives were greatly frightened. Then the captain-general had a man [wearing full armour] . . . placed . . . in the midst of three men armed with swords and daggers, who struck him on all parts of the body. Thereby was the king rendered almost speechless.

The captain-general told him through the slave that one of those armed men was worth one hundred of his own men. The king answered that that was a fact. The captain-general said that he had two hundred men in each ship who were armed in that manner. He showed the king cuirasses, swords, and bucklers, and had a review made for him.

Then he led the king to the deck of the ship, that is located above at the stern; and had his sea chart and compass brought. He told the king through the interpreter how he had found the strait in order to voyage thither, and how many moons he had been without seeing land, whereat the king was astonished. Lastly, he told the king that he would like, if it were pleasing to him, to send two of his men with him so that he might show them some of his things. The king replied that he was agreeable, and I went in company with one of the other men.

Magellan's statement that he had 200 men in each ship was highly exaggerated. He wished to impress the king with Spanish power. The entire fleet contained fewer than 300 at the start of the voyage (see p. 18). By now the *San Antonio*, with more than 60 men, had deserted, 19 men had died of scurvy, and others had been lost in the mutiny and in skirmishes in South America. Magellan's force was reduced to not many more than 150 men.

ANTONIO AS AMBASSADOR

Antonio Pigafetta's companion on his trip to Limasaua as ambassador was the slave Enrique de Malacca, his interpreter. First the Rajah Colambu gave them drinks on his royal *balanghai*, or barge. Then he banqueted them at his "palace," a typical Filipino house of bamboo and thatch, raised high above the earth on piles because of the rainy season.

Such houses are found in the Philippines today. They contain from one to three rooms. Openings covered by stiff bamboo mats serve as windows or doors, and the roof is of heavy bamboo matting topped with nipa thatch. The space below the house is often partly enclosed, serving as a chicken coop or for storage.

When I reached shore, the king raised his hands toward the sky and then turned toward us two. We did the same toward him as did all the others. The king took me by the hand; one of his chiefs took my companion: and thus they led us under a bamboo covering, where there was a *balanghai*, as long as eighty of my palm lengths, and resembling a *fusta* [cargo vessel]. We sat down upon the stern of that *balanghai*, constantly conversing with signs. The king's men stood about us in a circle with swords, daggers, spears, and bucklers.

The king had a plate of pork brought in and a large jar filled with wine. . . . I ate meat on [Good] Friday, for I could not help myself. Before the supper hour I gave the king many things which I had brought. I wrote down the names of many things in their language. When the king and the others saw me writing, and when I told them their words, they were all astonished. . . .

After [supper] we went to the palace of the king

which was built like a hayloft and was thatched with fig [banana] and palm leaves. It was built up high from the ground on huge posts of wood and it was necessary to ascend to it by means of ladders. The king made us sit down there on a bamboo mat with our feet drawn up like tailors. After a half-hour a platter of roast fish cut in pieces was brought in, and ginger freshly gathered, and wine. . . .

My companion became intoxicated as a consequence of so much drinking and eating. . . . [Then] the king made us a sign that he was going to go to sleep. He left the prince with us, and we slept with the latter on a bamboo mat with pillows made of leaves.

When day dawned the king came and took me by the hand, and in that manner we went to where we had had supper, in order to partake of refreshments, but the boat came to get us. Before we left, the king kissed our hands with great joy, and we his. One of his brothers, the king of another island, and three men came with us. The captain-general kept him to dine with us, and gave him many things. . . .

The name of the first king is Rajah Colambu, and the second [his brother] Rajah Siaui.

ON THE HIGHEST MOUNTAIN

In the Philippines a distinct change came over Magellan. Portuguese and Spaniards voyaged with the cross of Christ painted on their sails, seeking converts as well as trade. But now the captain-general, who had always been devout, made the spreading of Christianity his chief concern. He invited the two rajahs to his Easter Mass and spoke glowingly of the benefits to be received from a cross placed on their highest mountain.

Further, he rejected a plea of his officers to sail directly to the Spice Islands. When the captains reminded him that those were the king's orders, and when Juan Serrano spoke anxiously of his brother Francisco, Magellan's good friend, waiting there, Magellan replied that he had a secret understanding with Charles V to explore the Philippines. He was obsessed with his dream of converting the natives and making this splendid archipelago a Spanish bastion in the Pacific.

Early on the morning of Sunday, the last of March, and Easter day, the captain-general sent the priest with some men to prepare the place where mass was to be said; together with the interpreter to tell the king that we were not going to land in order to dine with him, but to say mass. Therefore the king sent us two swine that he had had killed.

When the hour for mass arrived, we landed with about fifty men, without our body armour, but carrying our other arms, and dressed in our best clothes. Before we reached the shore with our boats, six pieces were discharged as a sign of peace. We landed; the two kings embraced the captain-general, and placed him between them. We went in marching order to the place consecrated, which was not far from the shore . . . [and] the mass was offered up. . . .

The captain-general arranged a fencing tournament, at which the kings were greatly pleased. Then he had a cross carried in and the nails and a crown, to which immediate reverence was made. He told the kings through the interpreter that they were the standards given to him by the emperor his sovereign, so that wherever he might go he might set up those his tokens.

He said that he wished to set it up in that place for their benefit, for whenever any of our ships came, they would know that we had been there by that cross, and would do nothing to displease them or harm their property. If any of their men were captured, they would be set free immediately on that sign being shown.

It was necessary to set that cross on the summit of the highest mountain, so that on seeing it every morning, they might adore it; and if they did that, neither thunder, lightning, nor storms would harm them in the least. They thanked him heartily and said that they would do everything willingly.

The captain-general also had them asked whether they were Moors or heathen, or what was their belief. They replied that they worshipped nothing, but that they raised their clasped hands and their face to the sky; and that they called their god "Abba." Thereat the captain was very glad, and seeing that, the first king raised his hands to the sky, and said that he wished that it were possible for him to make the captain see his love for him. . . .

After dinner we all returned clad in our doublets, and that afternoon went together with the two kings to the summit of the highest mountain there. When we reached the summit, the captain-general told them that he esteemed highly having sweated for them, for since the cross was there, it could not but be of great use to them.

On asking them which port was the best to get food, they replied that there were three, namely, Leyte, Cebu, and Mindanao, but that Cebu was the largest and the one with most trade. They offered of their own accord to give us pilots to show us the way. The captain-general thanked them, and determined to go there, for so did his unhappy fate will.

In the end Rajah Colambu decided to be Magellan's pilot himself. Magellan had his men help the king harvest his rice before leaving his island of Limasaua. In some sentences omitted here Pigafetta also tells how the natives chewed betel nut, which "makes the mouth exceedingly red . . . [and] is very cooling to the heart." Betel nut stained their teeth black, too, and blackened teeth were considered a mark of beauty. No one wanted white teeth like a dog's!

VOYAGE TO CEBU

Upon learning that Cebu was the wealthiest, most populated land in the Philippines, Magellan sailed there. Cebu is a low, cigar-shaped island in the middle of the southern half of the archipelago. It is not much larger than Greater London; however, its importance was shown by the numerous villages and fishweirs lining its shore, the presence

of a Moorish (Arab) merchant at its court, and the boldness of its short, fat king, Rajah Humabon.

The queer black birds Pigafetta saw on the way are
known as mound builders; the fruit-eating bats are called
flying foxes.

We laid our course toward the northwest, passing
among five islands, namely, Leyte, Bohol, Canigao,
the northern part of Leyte, and Gatighan.

In the last-named island of Gatighan, there are bats
as large as eagles. As it was late we killed one of them,
which resembled chicken in taste. There are doves,
turtledoves, parrots, and certain black birds as large
as domestic chickens, which have a long tail. The last
mentioned birds lay eggs as large as the goose, and
bury them under the sand, through the great heat of
which they hatch out. When the chicks are born, they
push up the sand, and come out. Those eggs are good
to eat. . . .

At noon on Sunday, April 7, [1521], we entered
the port of Cebu, passing by many villages, where we
saw many houses built upon logs. On approaching the
city, the captain-general ordered the ships to fling
their banners. The sails were lowered and arranged as
if for battle, and all the artillery was fired, an action
which caused great fear to those people. The captain
sent a foster-son of his as ambassador to the king of
Cebu with the interpreter. . . .

The king told [the interpreter] that he was wel-

A parrot of the Philippines

come, but that it was their custom for all ships that entered their ports to pay tribute, and that it was but four days since a junk from Siam laden with gold and slaves had paid him tribute. As proof of his statement the king pointed out to the interpreter a merchant from Siam, who had remained to trade the gold and slaves.

The interpreter told the king that, since his master was the captain of so great a king, he did not pay tribute to any seignior in the world, and that if the king wished peace he would have peace, but if war instead, war. Thereupon, the Moorish merchant said to the king: "Look well, sire. These men are the same who have conquered Calicut, Malacca, and all India Major. If they are treated well, they will give good treatment, but if they are treated evil, evil and worse treatment, as they have done to Calicut and Malacca.". . .

The king . . . said thereupon that he would deliberate with his men, and would answer the captain on the following day. . . .

Monday morning, our notary, together with the interpreter, went to Cebu. The king, accompanied by his chiefs, came to the open square where he had our men sit down near him. He asked the notary whether there were more than one captain in that company, and whether that captain wished him to pay tribute to the emperor his master. The notary replied in the negative, but that the captain wished only to trade with him and with no others.

The king said that he was satisfied, and that if the captain wished to become his friend, he should send him a drop of blood from his right arm, and he himself would do the same to him as a sign of the most sincere friendship. The notary answered that the captain would do it.

MAGELLAN PREACHES CHRIST

Although Magellan fired his cannon to awe the natives, his one thought now was to make them his brothers in Christ. He, Antonio Pigafetta, and Father Valderrama, priest of the fleet, devoted themselves to saving pagan souls—so much so that the other officers criticized Magellan for neglecting trade and profits.

Magellan's reliance largely upon persuasion rather than force in his conversions contrasts with the practice of many early explorers. In spite of their stone crosses and protestations, the Portuguese and Spaniards had hitherto made few voluntary converts. Columbus, for example, imposed Christianity and slavery simultaneously upon the natives of Hispaniola.

After dinner the king's nephew, who was the prince, came to the ships with the king of Limasaua, the Moor, the governor, the chief constable, and eight chiefs, to make peace with us. The captain-general was seated in a red velvet chair, the principal men on leather chairs, and the others on mats upon the floor.

The captain-general asked them through the interpreter whether it were their custom to speak in secret or in public, and whether that prince and the king of Limasaua had authority to make peace. They answered that they spoke in public, and that they were empowered to make peace.

The captain-general said many things concerning peace, and that he prayed God to confirm it in heaven. . . . The captain told them that God made the sky, the earth, the sea, and everything else, and that He had commanded us to honour our fathers and mothers, and that whoever did otherwise was condemned to eternal fire; that we are all descended from Adam and Eve, our first parents; that we have an immortal spirit; and many other things pertaining to the faith. . . . He assured them that if they became Christians, the devil would no longer appear to them except in the last moment at their death.

They said that they could not answer the beautiful words of the captain, but that they placed themselves in his hands, and that he should treat them as his most faithful servants.

The captain embraced them weeping, and clasping one of the prince's hands and one of the king's between his own, said to them that, by his faith in God and to his sovereign, the emperor, and by the habit which he wore, he promised them that he would give them perpetual peace with the king of Spain. They answered that they promised the same. After the conclusion of the peace, the captain had refreshments served to them. . . .

Then he sent to the king of Cebu through me and one other a yellow and violet silk robe, made in Turkish style, a fine red cap, some strings of glass beads, all in a silver dish, and two gilt drinking cups in our hands.

When we reached the city we found the king in his palace surrounded by many people. He was seated on a palm mat on the ground, with . . . a scarf embroidered with the needle about his head, a necklace of great value hanging from his neck, and two large gold earrings fastened in his ears set round with precious gems.

He was fat and short, and tattooed with fire in various designs. From another mat on the ground he was eating turtle eggs which were in two porcelain dishes, and he had four jars full of palm wine in front of him covered with sweet-smelling herbs and arranged with four small reeds in each jar by means of which he drank.

Having duly made reverence to him, the interpreter told the king that his master thanked him very warmly for his present, and that he sent this present not in return for his present but for the intrinsic love which he bore him. We dressed him in the robe, placed the cap on his head, and gave him the other things; then kissing the beads and putting them upon his head, I presented them to him. He doing the same [kissing them] accepted them.

Then the king had us eat some of those eggs and

drink through those slender reeds. The others, his men, told him in that place, the words of the captain concerning peace and his exhortation to them to become Christians. The king wished to have us stay to supper with him, but we told him that we could not stay then.

Having taken our leave of him, the prince took us with him to his house, where four young girls were playing instruments—one, on a drum like ours, but resting on the ground; the second was striking two suspended gongs alternately with a stick wrapped somewhat thickly at the end with palm cloth; the third, one large gong in the same manner; and the last, two small gongs held in her hand, by striking one against the other, which gave forth a sweet sound. They played so harmoniously that one would believe they possessed good musical sense. Those girls were very beautiful and almost as white as our girls and as large. . . .

We took refreshments and then went to the ships. Those gongs are made of brass and are manufactured in the regions about the Great Gulf which is called China. They are used in those regions as we use bells and are called *aghon*.

ROYAL CONVERTS

The conversion of king, queen, and subjects described below was destined to last but a few days and to be followed by tragedy. Yet it was not in vain that the artillery crashed and the baptismal water was poured over the white-garmented king. The conversion of the Philippines begun here was completed by Legaspi and his Augustinian friars in 1565—a peaceful conquest without parallel in history, according to one scholar.

Even the wooden image of the Holy Child, given to the queen, survived and was found by Legaspi's Spanish soldiers. The natives called it "God."

Today the Philippines are the only Christian nation of Asia.

On Sunday morning, April 14, [1521], forty men of us went ashore, two of whom were completely armed and preceded the royal banner. When we reached land all the artillery was fired. Those people followed us hither and thither. The captain and the king embraced. . . . Then we all approached the platform joyfully.

The captain and the king sat down in chairs of red and violet velvet, the chiefs on cushions, and the others on mats. . . . The captain told the king that he was going to Spain, but that he would return again with so many forces that he would make him the greatest king of those regions, as he had been the first to express a determination to become a Christian.

The king, lifting his hands to the sky, thanked the captain, and requested him to let some of his men remain with him, so that he and his people might be better instructed in the faith. The captain replied that he would leave two men to satisfy him, but that he

would like to take two of the children of the chiefs
with him, so that they might learn our language, who
afterward on their return would be able to tell the
others the wonders of Spain. . . .

The captain led the king by the hand . . . in
order to baptize him. He told the king that he would
call him Don Carlos, after his sovereign the emperor.
. . . Five hundred men were baptized before mass.
After the conclusion of mass, the captain invited the
king and some of the other chiefs to dinner, but they
refused, accompanying us, however, to the shore. The
ships discharged all the mortars; and embracing, the
king and chiefs and the captain took leave of one another.

After dinner the priest and some of the others went
ashore to baptize the queen, who came with forty
women. We conducted her to the platform, and she
was made to sit down upon a cushion, and the other
women near her, until the priest should be ready. She
was shown an image of our Lady, a very beautiful
wooden child Jesus, and a cross. Thereupon, she was
overcome with contrition, and asked for baptism
amid her tears.

We named her Joanna, after the emperor's mother.
. . . Counting men, women, and children, we baptized eight hundred souls.

The queen was young and beautiful, and was entirely covered with a white and black cloth. Her
mouth and nails were very red, while on her head she

wore a large hat of palm leaves in the manner of a
parasol, with a crown about it of the same leaves, like
the tiara of the pope; and she never goes any place
without such a one. She asked us to give her the little
child Jesus to keep in place of her idols; and then she
went away.

In the afternoon, the king and queen, accompanied
by numerous persons, came to the shore. Thereupon,
the captain had many trombs [rocket tubes] of fire
and large mortars discharged, by which they were
most highly delighted. The captain and the king
called one another brothers. That king's name was
Rajah Humabon.

CHAPTER SIX

"SO NOBLE A CAPTAIN"

April 14, 1521 — May 1, 1521

Ferdinand Magellan desired that the other kings, neighbours to this one, should become subject to this who had become Christian: and these did not choose to yield such obedience.

—*The First Voyage Around the World,*
BY A GENOESE PILOT

MAGELLAN'S CHRISTIAN EMPIRE

Magellan hoped that these high volcanic islands, the Philippines, heavily forested from the tropical rains, with their blue waterways and brown people, would become an outpost for Christ and Spain. His chief lieutenant in building a Christian realm would be King Humabon, now baptized as the Rajah Charles. Magellan referred to him as "the Christian king" and ordered all the other chiefs to obey Humabon in his red velvet chair.

Pigafetta's narrative continues below.

Before mass one day, the captain-general had the king come clad in his silk robe, and the chief men of the city . . . and many others whom I shall not name in order not to be tedious. The captain made them all swear to be obedient to their king, and they kissed the latter's hand.

Then the captain had the king declare that he would always be obedient and faithful to the king of Spain, and the king so swore. Thereupon, the captain drew his sword before the image of our Lady, and told the king that when anyone so swore, he should prefer to die rather than to break such an oath. . . . After . . . that the captain gave the king a red velvet chair, telling him that wherever he went he should always have it carried before him by one of his nearest relatives; and he showed him how it ought to be carried.

The king responded that he would do that willingly for love of him.

A MIRACULOUS CURE

Magellan showed his continuing religious zeal by urging the natives to burn their idols. They hesitated to do this because they thought that idol worship and other superstitions helped cure disease. For example, they imagined a man might be cured of indigestion by having chicken blood and rice placed upon his stomach while a medium, in a trance, relayed further orders from the spirit world.

One day the captain-general asked the king and the other people why they did not burn their idols as they had promised when they became Christians; and why they sacrificed so much flesh to them. They replied that what they were doing was not for themselves, but for a sick man who had not spoken now for four days, so that the idols might give him health. He was the prince's brother, and the bravest and wisest man in the island.

The captain told them to burn their idols and to believe in Christ, and that if the sick man were baptized, he would quickly recover; and if that did not so happen they could behead him [Magellan] then and there. Thereupon, the king replied that he would do it, for he truly believed in Christ.

We made a procession from the square to the house of the sick man with as much pomp as possible. There we found him in such condition that he could neither speak nor move. We baptized him and his two wives, and ten girls. Then the captain had him asked how he felt. He spoke immediately and said that by the grace of our Lord he felt very well. . . .

Before five days the sick man began to walk. He had an idol that certain old women had concealed in his house burned in the presence of the king and all the people. He had many shrines along the seashore destroyed. . . . The people . . . said that if God would lend them life, they would burn all the idols that they could find. . . .

Those idols are made of wood, and are hollow, and lack the back parts. Their arms are open and their feet turned up under them with the legs open. They have a large face with four huge tusks like those of the wild boar; and are painted all over.

A REBEL ISLAND

The captain-general's threats cowed all the chiefs but one. Powerful King Cilapulapu of the small island of Mactan refused to attend Magellan's assembly of native leaders. "I will not abandon our worship of the gods, and I will make war on any chief who does," was Cilapulapu's message to Humabon.

When Cilapulapu defied King Humabon, Magellan sent a detachment of marines to burn Cilapulapu's capital, the town of Bulaia.

There are many villages in that island. . . . All those villages rendered obedience to us, and gave us food and tribute. Near that island of Cebu was an island called Mactan, which formed the port where we were anchored. The name of its village was Mactan, and its chiefs were Zula and Cilapulapu. We burned one hamlet which was located [in Mactan], because it refused to obey the king or us. We set up the cross there for those people were heathen. Had they been Moors, we would have erected a column there as a token of greater hardness, for the Moors are much harder to convert than the heathen. That city which we burned . . . was called Bulaia.

Afterward, Magellan demanded that Cilapulapu do homage to King Humabon and pay a tribute of swine, goats, fowl, rice, and coconuts.

Cilapulapu sullenly offered to send two-thirds of what was asked—"If Magellan was satisfied with this, they would at once comply; if not, it might be as he pleased, but they would not give him any more."

THE BATTLE OF MACTAN

Now Zula, a subchief on Mactan, also sent less than the requested tribute and blamed Cilapulapu for the shortage. Magellan determined to make an example of the rebel island, ignored his captains' pleas not to risk himself, and prepared for battle.

The captain-general looked upon the proposed skirmish as a crusade. He neglected many sensible precautions, such as using his own officers or trained marines, or accepting the help offered by King Humabon and Zula. Instead he took only sixty inexperienced volunteers and even let

Cilapulapu know exactly when he would attack. He invited King Humabon and his people to witness the triumph of Christian arms, supported by God.

At midnight [April 26, 1521], sixty men of us set out armed with corselets and helmets, together with the Christian king, the prince, some of the chief men, and twenty or thirty *balanghais*. We reached Mactan three hours before dawn. The captain did not wish to fight then, but sent a message to the natives by the Moor to the effect that if they would obey the king of Spain, recognize the Christian king as their sovereign, and pay us our tribute, he would be their friend; but that if they wished otherwise, they should wait to see how our lances wounded.

They replied that if we had lances they had lances of bamboo and stakes hardened with fire. They asked us not to proceed to attack them at once, but to wait until morning, so that they might have more men. They said that in order to induce us to go in search of them; for they had dug certain pitholes between the houses in order that we might fall into them.

When morning came forty-nine of us leaped into the water up to our thighs, and walked through water for more than two crossbow flights before we could reach the shore. The boats could not approach nearer because of certain rocks in the water. The other eleven men remained behind to guard the boats.

When we reached land, those men had formed in three divisions to the number of more than one thousand five hundred persons. When they saw us, they charged down upon us with exceeding loud cries, two divisions on our flanks and the other on our front. When the captain saw that, he formed us into two divisions, and thus did we begin to fight.

The musketeers and crossbowmen shot from a distance for about a half-hour, but uselessly. . . . The captain cried to them, "Cease firing! Cease firing!" but his order was not at all heeded.

When the natives saw that we were shooting our muskets to no purpose . . . they redoubled their shouts [and] . . . determined to stand firm. When our muskets were discharged, the natives would never stand still, but leaped hither and thither, covering themselves with their shields. They shot so many arrows at us and hurled so many bamboo spears (some of them tipped with iron) at the captain-general, besides pointed stakes hardened with fire, stones, and mud, that we could scarcely defend ourselves.

Seeing that, the captain-general sent some men to burn their houses in order to terrify them. When they saw their houses burning, they were roused to greater fury. Two of our men were killed near the houses, while we burned twenty or thirty houses.

So many of them charged down upon us that they shot the captain [Magellan] through the right leg with a poisoned arrow. On that account, he ordered us to retire slowly, but the men took to flight, except six or eight of us who remained with the captain.

The natives shot only at our legs, for the latter were bare; and so many were the spears and stones that they hurled at us, that we could offer no resistance. The mortars in the boats could not aid us as they were too far away. So we continued to retire for more than a good crossbow flight from the shore always fighting up to our knees in the water.

The natives continued to pursue us, and picking up the same spear four or six times, hurled it at us again and again. Recognizing the captain, so many turned upon him that they knocked his helmet off his head twice, but he always stood firmly like a good knight, together with some others.

Thus did we fight for more than one hour, refusing to retire farther. An Indian hurled a bamboo spear into the captain's face, but the latter immediately killed him with his lance, which he left in the Indian's body. Then, trying to lay hand on sword, he could draw it but halfway, because he had been wounded in the arm with a bamboo spear.

When the natives saw that, they all hurled themselves upon him. One of them wounded him on the left leg with a large cutlass, which resembles a scimitar, only being larger. That caused the captain to fall face downward, when immediately they rushed upon him with iron and bamboo spears and with their cutlasses, until they killed our mirror, our light, our comfort, and our true guide.

When they wounded him, he turned back many

F*

The death of Magellan at the battle of Mactan, 152

(From De Bry's *Americae IX*, 1602)

times to see whether we were all in the boats. Thereupon, beholding him dead, we, wounded, retreated as best we could to the boats, which were already pulling off. The Christian king [Humabon] would have aided us, but the captain charged him before we landed not to leave his *balanghai* but to stay to see how we fought. When the king learned that the captain was dead, he wept.

THE CHARACTER OF MAGELLAN

Had it not been for that unfortunate captain, not a single one of us would have been saved in the boats, for while he was fighting the others retired to the boats. I hope . . . that the fame of so noble a captain will not become effaced in our times.

Among the other virtues which he possessed, he was more constant than ever any one else in the greatest of adversity. He endured hunger better than all the others, and more accurately than any man in the world did he understand sea charts and navigation. And that this was the truth was seen openly, for no other had had so much natural talent nor the boldness to learn how to circumnavigate the world, as he had almost done.

That battle was fought on Saturday, April 27, 1521. The captain desired to fight on Saturday, because it was the day especially holy to him. Eight of our men were killed with him in that battle, and four

Indians, who had become Christians and who had come afterward to aid us were killed by the mortars of the boats. Of the enemy, only fifteen were killed, while many of us were wounded.

The mortars referred to above had been fired by the Spaniards left in the boats offshore, beyond the "rocks" (coral reefs). They were trying to cover Magellan's retreat; unfortunately, fragments of their missiles struck their allies, King Humabon's warriors.

Like so many of his countrymen, Magellan fell far from home, his burial place unknown. God gave the Portuguese a small land for their birthplace, said a missionary, but all the world to die in.

AFTERMATH

After the loss of their leader, Magellan's men were fearful and confused. Instead of attacking again, in full force, to avenge their captain-general, they weakly asked for Magellan's body. Their request was refused.

Then they revealed their distrust of their ally, King Humabon, by hastily removing all their goods—knives, copper, cotton cloth, bells, combs, etc.—from his village, piling them into longboats and taking them back to the ships.

Meanwhile King Humabon, who had helped the survivors escape from the pursuing canoes of Cilapulapu, was under great pressure. Cilapulapu offered him friendship if he would join in driving out the foreigners; otherwise Cilapulapu threatened to head an alliance of native chiefs against Humabon.

At this point Magellan's Enrique de Malacca, the expedition's interpreter, turned against the Spaniards. Together he and King Humabon devised a trap which the new leaders of the fleet walked into blindly.

On Saturday, the day on which the captain was killed, the four men who had remained in the city to trade, had our merchandise carried to the ships. Then we chose two commanders, namely, Duarte Barbosa . . . and Juan Serrano. . . .

As our interpreter, Enrique by name, was wounded slightly, he would not go ashore any more to attend to our necessary affairs, but always kept to his bed. On that account, Duarte Barbosa, the commander of the flagship, cried out to him and told him, that although his master, the captain, was dead, he was not therefore free; on the contrary he [Barbosa] would see to it that when we should reach Spain, he should still be the slave of Doña Beatriz, the wife of the captain-general.

And threatening the slave that if he did not go ashore, he would be flogged, the latter arose, and, feigning to take no heed to those words, went ashore to tell the Christian king that we were about to leave very soon, but that if he would follow his advice, he could gain the ships and all our merchandise. Accordingly they arranged a plot, and the slave returned to the ship, where he showed that he was more cunning than before.

On Wednesday morning, May 1, [1521], the Christian king sent word to the commanders that the jewels which he had promised to send to the king of Spain were ready, and that he begged them and their other companions to come to dine with him that morning, when he would give them the jewels. Twenty-four men went ashore, among whom was our astrologer, San Martín of Seville. I could not go because I was all swollen up by a wound from a poisoned arrow which I had received in my face.

Juan Carvalho and the constable [Espinosa] returned, and told us that . . . they had left that place, because they suspected some evil.

Scarcely had they spoken those words when we heard loud cries and lamentations. We immediately weighed anchor and discharging many mortars into the houses, drew in nearer to the shore. While thus discharging our pieces we saw Juan Serrano in his shirt bound and wounded, crying to us not to fire any more, for the natives would kill him.

We asked him whether all the others and the interpreter were dead. He said that they were all dead except the interpreter. He begged us earnestly to redeem him with some of the merchandise; but Juan Carvalho, his boon companion, and others would not allow the boat to go ashore so that they might remain masters of the ships.

But although Juan Serrano weeping asked us not

to set sail so quickly, for they would kill him, and said that he prayed God to ask his soul of Juan Carvalho, his comrade, in the day of judgment, we immediately departed. I do not know whether he is dead.

CHAPTER SEVEN

THE SPICE ISLANDS

May 1, 1521 — December 11, 1521

We went S.S.E. until we sighted the Moluccas, and then we went to East, and entered between Mare and Tidore, at which we anchored, and there we were very well received, and made very good arrangements for peace, and made a house on shore for trading with the people, and so we remained many days, until we had taken in cargo.

—The Log-Book of Francisco Albo

THE BURNING OF THE *CONCEPCIÓN*

Through the treachery of King Humabon the fleet had lost twenty-two more men, including the experienced Serrano and Barbosa, who had been elected together to succeed Magellan. Their total number was now only 115—less than half the men who had originally sailed from Seville.

This remnant burned the leaky *Concepción*, chose Carvalho as their new captain-general, and made Espinosa captain of the *Victoria*, replacing the slain Barbosa. Then early in May, 1521, they blundered off toward the Moluccas—in the wrong direction.

Pigafetta's narrative continues below.

In the midst of that archipelago, at a distance of eighteen leagues from [the] island of Cebu, at the head of the other island called Bohol, we burned the ship *Concepción,* for too few men of us were left to work it. We stowed the best of its contents in the other two ships [*Trinidad* and *Victoria*], and then laid our course toward the south southwest.

Sailing west instead of south, they turned a two weeks' voyage into a six months' odyssey of hunger, piracy, and frustration.

"We were often on the point of abandoning the ships and going ashore in order that we might not die of hunger," wrote Pigafetta.

When they had only eight days' provisions left, they came to Palawan, westernmost of the Philippines, and were given pigs, goats, poultry, fruits, and rice by the generous ruler. In return for this food, which saved their lives, the Spaniards later captured the Palawan king and held him for a huge ransom!

Now they sailed on, southwest toward Borneo.

IN THE VENICE OF THE EAST

As the fleet neared its destination the people encountered became less savage, more languid, exotic, and oriental. At Brunei, chief city of Borneo, Magellan's men did obeisance to a great warrior-sultan in his luxurious court. A population larger than the present one spread out in houses built above the water on palm piles.

From their anchorage at the mouth of the Brunei River, the Europeans—the first white men to visit Brunei—looked at the houses built over the water and the palaces on land toward a background of cleared hills and distant heights clothed with dense green forest. They saw nearby another city, also built over the water, inhabited by "heathens," and learned of daily naval battles between Mohammedan Brunei and this city.

Brunei, also called "City of Peace," was a wealthy trading centre. Pigafetta saw the daily market carried on at high tide right on the lake-like river by a dense pack of canoes, with the shrill cries of the women, in their enormous hats, echoing over the water.

Much of the shipping consisted of junks. As Pigafetta observed, this remarkable vessel had a cargo capacity equal to that of much larger European ships. It had square sails of fibre matting and a flat-bottomed pontoon hull. The hull was divided into many watertight compartments, each entered by its own hatch from the row of hatches on the flat deck above.

Borneo is the third largest island in the world. Camphor was its most valuable product.

When we reached the city [of Brunei, in Borneo], we remained about two hours in the prau [a small, lateen-sail boat], until the arrival of two elephants

with silk trappings, and twelve men each of whom
carried a porcelain jar covered with silk in which to
carry our presents. Thereupon, we mounted the elephants while those twelve men preceded us afoot
with the presents in the jars. In this way we went to
the house of the governor. . . .

Next day . . . we went to the king's palace upon
elephants, with our presents in front as on the preceding day. . . . We went up a ladder . . . and entered a large hall full of many nobles, where we sat
down upon a carpet with the presents in the jars
near us.

At the end of that hall there is another hall higher
but somewhat smaller. . . . At the end of the small
hall was a large window from which a brocade curtain
was drawn aside so that we could see within it the
king seated at a table with one of his young sons
chewing betel. No one but women were behind him.

Then a chief told us that we could not speak to the
king, and that if we wished anything, we were to tell
it to him, so that he could communicate it to one of
higher rank. The latter would communicate it to a
brother of the governor who was stationed in the
smaller hall, and this man would communicate it by
means of a speaking-tube through a hole in the wall
to one who was inside with the king.

The chief taught us the manner of making three
obeisances to the king with our hands clasped above

the head, raising first one foot and then the other and then kissing the hands toward him, and we did so. . . .

We told the king that we came from the king of Spain, and that the latter desired to make peace with him and asked only for permission to trade. The king had us told that since the king of Spain desired to be his friend, he was very willing to be his, and said that we could take water and wood, and trade at our pleasure.

Then we gave him the presents, on receiving each of which he nodded slightly. To each one of us was given some brocaded and gold cloth and silk, which were placed upon our left shoulders, where they were left but a moment. They presented us with refreshments of cloves and cinnamon, after which the curtains were drawn to and the windows closed. The men in the palace were all attired in cloth of gold and silk . . . and carried daggers with gold hafts adorned with pearls and precious gems, and they had many rings on their hands. . . .

That city is entirely built [over] salt water, except the houses of the king and certain chiefs. It contains twenty-five thousand fires [families]. The houses are all constructed of wood and built up from the ground on tall pillars. When the tide is high the women go in boats through the settlement selling the articles necessary to maintain life.

There is a large brick wall in front of the king's house with towers like a fort, in which were mounted fifty-six bronze pieces, and six of iron. During the two days of our stay there, many pieces were discharged. . . .

On Monday morning, July 29, [1521], we saw more than one hundred praus divided into three squadrons and a like number of *tunguli* (which are their small boats) coming toward us. . . . Imagining that there was some trickery afoot, we hoisted our sails as quickly as possible. . . . We expected especially that we were to be captured in between certain junks which had anchored behind us. . . . We immediately turned upon the latter, capturing four of them and killing many persons. . . .

In that same port there is another city inhabited by heathens, which is larger than that of the Moors, and built like the latter [over] salt water. On that account the two peoples have daily combats together in that same harbour. . . . When the Moorish king heard how we had treated the junks, he sent us a message . . . that the praus were not coming to do us any harm, but that they were going to attack the heathens. . . .

We sent a message to the king, asking him to please allow two of our men who were in the city . . . to come to us, but the king refused. . . . We kept sixteen of the chiefest men of the captured junks to take them to Spain, and three women in the queen's name, but Juan Carvalho usurped the latter for himself.

JUNKS, PEARLS, AND CAMPHOR

[In Borneo] junks are their ships and are made in the following manner. The bottom part is built about two palms above the water and is of planks fastened with wooden pegs, which are very well made; above that they are entirely made of very large bamboos. They have a bamboo as a counterweight. One of those junks carries as much cargo as a ship. Their masts are of bamboo, and the sails of the bark of trees.

Their porcelain is a sort of exceedingly white earth which is left for fifty years under the earth before it is worked, for otherwise it would not be fine. The father buries it for the son. If poison is placed in a dish made of fine porcelain, the dish immediately breaks. . . .

At that place the people highly esteem bronze, quicksilver, glass, cinnabar, wool cloth, linens, and all our other merchandise, although iron and spectacles more than all the rest. Those Moors go naked as do the other peoples of those regions. They drink quicksilver—the sick man drinks it to cleanse himself, and the well man to preserve his health.

The king of Borneo has two pearls as large as two hen's eggs. They are so round that they will not stand still on a table. I know that for a fact, for when we carried the king's presents to him, signs were made for him to show them to us, but he said that he would show them next day. Afterward some chiefs said that they had seen them. . . .

Camphor, a kind of balsam, is produced in that island. It exudes between the wood and the bark, and the drops are as small as grains of wheat bran. If it is exposed it gradually evaporates. Those people call it *capor*. Cinnamon, ginger, . . . oranges, lemons, . . . watermelons, cucumbers, gourds, turnips, cabbages, scallions [onions], cows, buffaloes, swine, goats, chicken, geese, deer, elephants, horses, and other things are found there.

After leaving Brunei, Magellan's men sailed back toward the Philippines, looking for a harbour in which to careen and repair the ships. Among some islands off north Borneo they found a port which they named Port St. Mary, where they overhauled and calked the *Trinidad* and *Victoria*. To obtain timbers, the shoeless sailors had to walk over thorns and briars in the forest.

Here Carvalho was deprived of his command. Sturdy Espinosa, the chief of marines, was elected captain-general; Sebastián del Cano, involved in the mutiny at St. Julian but probably the best navigator left, was made captain of the *Victoria*.

ARRIVAL AT THE MOLUCCAS

For several weeks the two ships could not find the Moluccas. Magellan's men wandered all the way back to the Philippines, practising piracy en route. Then, with the aid of some captured pilots, they headed south and finally reached the fabled Spice Islands.

The Moluccas, wrote Pigafetta, consist of "Ternate, Tidore, Mortier, and Makian . . . four lofty and peaked mountains [islands] where the cloves grow," and a fifth island, Bachian, "[whose] clove mountain is not so sharp as the others, but . . . is larger." The natives had been converted to Mohammedanism about fifty years before. In addition to their spices—cloves, ginger, nutmeg—the islands produced "rice, goats, geese, chickens, coconuts, figs [bananas], almonds . . . pomegranates, oranges, lemons, camotes [sweet potatoes], honey . . . sugar cane" and other foods as well as red and white parrots. These islands were crowned by volcanoes.

In the Moluccas the Spaniards, coming from the west, ran head-on into the Portuguese, who had arrived from the east (from India and the Malay Peninsula). Magellan himself had taken part in the two expeditions against Malacca, in 1509 and 1511, which spearheaded the Portuguese advance to the East Indies. Now Magellan's men learned that the Portuguese sent junks annually from Malacca to the Spice Islands to trade, and that a small Portuguese force had only recently been massacred on Bachian. At any moment the Portuguese might return to Ternate, where Francisco Serrano had been given permission to build a fortress, and enforce their claim to the Moluccas.

On Wednesday, November 6, [1521], we discovered four lofty islands. . . . The pilot who still remained with us told us that those four islands were the Moluccas. Therefore, we thanked God and as an expression of our joy discharged all our artillery. It was no wonder that we were so glad, for we had passed twenty-seven months less two days in our search for the Moluccas. . . .

Three hours before sunset on Friday, November

THE SPICE ISLANDS   [151]

8, 1521, we entered into a harbour of an island called Tidore, and anchoring near the shore in twenty fathoms we fired all our artillery.

Next day the king came to the ships in a prau, and circled about them once. We immediately went to meet him in a small boat, in order to show him honour. He made us enter his prau and seat ourselves near him. He was seated under a silk awning which sheltered him on all sides. In front of him was one of his sons with the royal sceptre, and two persons with two gold jars to pour water on his hands, and two others with two gilded caskets filled with their betel.

The king told us that we were welcome there, and that he had dreamt some time ago that some ships were coming to the Moluccas from remote parts; and that for more assurance he had determined to consult the moon, whereupon he had seen the ships were coming, and that we were they.

Upon the king entering our ships all kissed his hand and then we led him to the stern. When he entered inside there, he would not stoop, but entered from above. Causing him to sit down in a red velvet chair, we clothed him in a yellow velvet robe made in the Turkish fashion. In order to show him greater honour, we sat down on the ground near him.

Then when all were seated, the king began to speak and said that he and all his people desired ever to be the most loyal friends and vassals to our king of Spain. He received us as his children, and we could go ashore as if in our own houses, for from that time thence-

fol. 64

Magellan's men arrive a

ccas (From De Bry's *Americae V*, 1595)

forth, his island was to be called no more Tidore but Castile, because of the great love which he bore to our king, his sovereign.

We made him a present which consisted of the robe, the chair, a piece of delicate linen, seven yards of scarlet cloth, a piece of brocaded silk, a piece of yellow damask, some Indian cloth embroidered with gold and silk, a piece of *berania* (the white linen of Cambay), two caps, six strings of glass beads, twelve knives, three large mirrors, six pairs of scissors, six combs, some gilded drinking cups, and other articles.

To his son we gave an Indian cloth of gold and silk, a large mirror, a cap, and two knives; and to each of nine others—all of them his chiefs—a silk cloth, caps, and two knives; and to many others caps or knives. We kept giving presents until the king bade us desist.

After that he declared to us that he had nothing else except his own life to send to the king his sovereign. We were to approach nearer to the city, and whoever came to the ships at night, we were to kill with our muskets. In leaving the stern, the king would never bend his head. When he took his leave we discharged all the guns.

That king is a Moor and about forty-five years old. He is well built and has a royal presence, and is an excellent astrologer. At that time he was clad in a shirt of the most delicate white stuff with the ends of the sleeves embroidered in gold, and in a cloth that reached from his waist to the ground. He was barefoot, and had a silk scarf wrapped about his head, and above it a garland of flowers. His name is Rajah Sultan Almanzor.

Rajah Almanzor proved to be a very helpful host. He not only welcomed Magellan's men warmly but promised to journey to the neighbouring island of Bachian to obtain more cloves for them because "there were not enough dry cloves in his island to load the two ships."

Apparently Almanzor feared the assistance which the Portuguese could give his old enemy, the king of Ternate. Almanzor wanted the Spaniards as future allies. He quickly signed a treaty acknowledging the sovereignty of Spain over his island and asked for one of Charles V's royal banners and his signature. Magellan's men, anxious to load their spices and depart, encouraged Almanzor's friendship.

THE FATE OF MAGELLAN'S FRIEND

Where was Francisco Serrano? In 1511 Magellan's cousin and companion in the East had sailed from Malacca, Portugal's easternmost base at that time, under Antonio de Abreu, commander of an expedition to discover the Spice Islands. After many adventures, including ship-burning and marooning, Serrano and his crew alone reached their goal. Abreu never got to the Moluccas. Serrano became the general and adviser of the king of Ternate, made him supreme over the king of Tidore, and exercised great influence in the Spice Islands.

Now, the Spaniards learned, Francisco Serrano was dead.

At that time it was not eight months since one Francisco Serrano had died in Ternate. He was a

Portuguese and the captain-general of the king of Ternate and opposed the king of Tidore. He did so well that he constrained the king of Tidore to give one of his daughters to wife to the king of Ternate, and almost all the sons of the chiefs as hostages. The . . . grandson of the king of Tidore was born to that daughter.

Peace having been made between the two kings, and when Francisco Serrano came one day to Tidore to trade cloves, the king of Tidore had him poisoned with . . . betel leaves. . . .

He was a close friend and a relative of our royal captain-general [Magellan], and was the cause of inciting the latter to undertake that enterprise, for when our captain was at Malacca, he had written to him several times that he was in Ternate. As Don Manuel, then king of Portugal, refused to increase our captain-general's pension by only a single testoon per month for his merits, the latter went to Spain, where he had obtained everything for which he could ask from his sacred Majesty [Charles V].

When Magellan's men asked a Portuguese from Ternate —what was the news back in Christendom?—they discovered that *they* were a big part of that news. King Manuel of Portugal had sent fleets to the Cape of Good Hope and to the Rio de la Plata, in South America, to destroy them! When these ships failed to encounter Magellan's expedition, King Manuel ordered six Portuguese ships from India to attack the Spaniards in the Moluccas.

However, the Portuguese ships were needed against the Arabs and never came.

HOW THE CLOVE GROWS

The clove trees described below are beautiful evergreens, thirty to forty feet high. The cloves themselves are unopened flower buds which grow in crimson clusters at the ends of branches. Half an inch long, the clove resembles a nail ("clove" comes from French *clou*, meaning "nail"); it has a strong, fragrant odour. Cloves were the most costly of all spices in the sixteenth-century European market.

Ginger and nutmeg were also found in the Moluccas, but the specialty was cloves, which then grew only in these islands.

On Friday, November 15, [1521], the king told us that he was going to [the island of] Bachian to get the cloves abandoned there by the Portuguese. . . .

[On Sunday] I went ashore to see how the clove grows. The clove tree is tall and as thick as a man's body or thereabout. Its branches spread out somewhat widely in the middle, but at the top they have the shape of a summit. Its leaves resemble those of the laurel, and the bark is of a dark colour.

The cloves grow at the end of the twigs, ten or twenty in a cluster. Those trees have generally more cloves on one side than on the other, according to the season. When the cloves sprout they are white, when ripe, red, and when dried, black.

They are gathered twice per year, once at the

nativity of our Saviour, and the other at the nativity
of St. John the Baptist; for the climate is more mod-
erate at those two seasons, but more so at the time of
the nativity of our Saviour. When the year is very hot
and there is little rain, those people gather three or
four hundred *bahars* [casks] of cloves in each of
those islands.

Those trees grow only in the mountains, and if any
of them are planted in the lowlands near the mountains, they do not live. The leaves, the bark, and the
green wood are as strong as the cloves. If the latter
are not gathered when they are ripe, they become
large and so hard that only their husk is good.

No cloves are grown in the world except in the five
mountains of those five islands, except that some are
found in Gilolo and in a small island between Tidore
and Mortier, by name Mare, but they are not good.
Almost every day we saw a mist descend and encircle
now one and now another of those mountains, on account of which those cloves become perfect. Each of
those people possesses clove trees, and each one
watches over his own trees although he does not cultivate them.

A SUSPICIOUS INVITATION

When Rajah Almanzor returned from the neighbouring
island of Bachian, he extended an invitation which made
Magellan's men remember Rajah Humabon, in the Philippines, and his treachery.

On Sunday night, November 24, [1521], and toward Monday, the king came [back] with gongs a-playing, and passed between the ships, whereat we discharged many pieces. He told us that cloves would be brought in quantity within four days. . . .

On Tuesday . . . the king . . . told us that it was the custom, when the first cloves were laden in the ships or in the junks, for the king to make a feast for the crews of the ships, and to pray their God that He would lead those ships safe to their port. He also wished to do it because of the king of Bachian and one of his brothers who were coming to visit him. . . .

Some of us imagining that some treachery was afoot . . . declared in opposition to some who wished to go to the feast that we ought not go ashore for feasts, for we remembered that other so unfortunate one. We were so urgent that it was concluded to send a message to the king asking him to come soon to the ships, for we were about to depart. . . .

The king came immediately and entered the ships. . . . He told us . . . that he had not left the island to do us any harm, but to supply the ships with cloves sooner. . . .

Then he had his Koran brought, and . . . declared in the presence of all, that he swore by Allah and by the Koran which he had in his hand, that he would always be a faithful friend to the king of Spain. He spoke all those words nearly in tears. In return for his

good words, we promised to wait another fortnight. . . .

None the less we heard afterward on good authority that some of the chiefs of those islands had
proposed to him to kill us, saying it would be doing
the greatest kind of pleasure to the Portuguese. . . .
But the king had replied that he would not do it
under any consideration, since he had recognized the
king of Spain and had made peace with him.

TRADING FOR SPICES

As pointed out in the Introduction, spices sold in Europe
for as much as 10,000 per cent of their price in the Moluccas. The spices brought back in just one ship, the *Victoria*,
paid all expenses of the fleet for three years, with a hand-
some profit left over for King Charles and Magellan's fi-
nancial backers. The cargo was worth well over half a
million dollars—about $675,000.

The standard measure of cloves, a *bahar*, was 406
pounds; *bahar* is sometimes translated "barrel" or "cask."

After dinner on Wednesday, November 27,
[1521], the king had an edict proclaimed that all
those who had cloves could bring them to the ships.
All that and the next day we bartered for cloves with
might and main . . . in the following manner.

For eighteen yards of red cloth of very good
quality, they gave us one *bahar* of cloves . . . ; for
fifteen hatchets, one *bahar;* for thirty-five glass

drinking cups, one *bahar* (the king getting them all);
for twenty-three pounds of cinnabar, one *bahar*; for
twenty-three pounds of quicksilver, one *bahar*; for
forty-eight yards of linen, one *bahar*; for forty-six
yards of finer linen, one *bahar*; for one hundred and
fifty knives, one *bahar*; for fifty pairs of scissors, one
bahar; for forty caps, one *bahar*; for ten pieces of
Guzerat cloth, one *bahar*; for three of those gongs of
theirs, two *bahars*. . . .

Almost all the mirrors were broken, and the few
good ones the king wished for himself. Many of those
things that we traded were from the above-mentioned
junks which he had captured. Our haste to return to
Spain made us dispose of our merchandise at better
bargains to the natives than we should have done.

Finally, when we had no more merchandise, one
man gave his cloak, another his doublet, and another
his shirt, besides other articles of clothing, in order
that they might have their share in the cargo. . . .

Several days later our king told us that he was like
a child at the breast who knew his dear mother, who
departing would leave him alone. Especially would he
be disconsolate, because now he had become ac-
quainted with us, and enjoyed some of the products
of Spain. Inasmuch as our return would be far in the
future, he earnestly entreated us to leave him some of
our culverins [muskets] for his defence.

He advised us to sail only by day when we left,
because of the numerous shoals amid those islands.

We replied to him that if we wished to reach Spain we would have to sail day and night. Thereupon, he told us that he would pray daily to his God for us, asking Him to conduct us in safety.

In spite of the success of Magellan's men in reaching the Moluccas, Spain was not destined to wrest control of these islands from Portugal. Several later expeditions failed, and in 1529 Charles V sold his claim to the Moluccas to Portugal for $5,000,000. Spain's penetration into the Pacific stopped where Magellan fell—in the Philippines.

CHAPTER EIGHT

AROUND THE WORLD

December 11, 1521 — September 8, 1522

September, 1522. On the 4th of the said month, in the morning, we saw land, and it was Cape St. Vincent [Portugal].

—The Log-Book of Francisco Albo

BIRD OF PARADISE

By December, 1521, it was time to leave the Moluccas. The men bent new sails adorned with the cross of St. James to their ships. They were eager to depart—yet they were also sad.

"What need is there of many words?" wrote Maximilian of Transylvania about the Spice Islands. "Everything there is humble and of no value, save peace, ease, and spices. The best and noblest of these, and the greatest possible good, namely, peace, seemed to have been driven by men's wickedness from our world to theirs."

So it had proved for Magellan's men, warmly welcomed by the king of Tidore and given an abundance of valuable cloves in trade. Now three more kings came forward to sign treaties of loyalty to Charles V.

One present brought by the king of Bachian summed up the romance and mystery of the East. It was "two extremely beautiful dead birds"—skins of the bird of paradise. As Maximilian related the legend of the bird for Europe, it was born in paradise, spent its life in perpetual flight, and plummeted to earth only at death. Its skins and plumes, a regular article of commerce, were said to render the wearer invincible in battle.

Pigafetta's narrative continues below.

[On Monday, December 16, 1521], we bent the new sails in the ships. On them was a cross of St. James of Galicia, with an inscription which read: "This is the sign of our good fortune."

On Tuesday, we gave our king [Almanzor of Tidore] certain pieces of artillery resembling arquebuses, which we had captured among those India islands, and some of our culverins, together with four barrels of powder. We took aboard at that place eighty butts of water in each ship. Five days previously the king had sent one hundred men to cut wood for us at the island of Mare, by which we were to pass.

On that day the king of Bachian and many of his men came ashore to make peace with us. Before the king walked four men with drawn daggers in their hands. In the presence of our king and of all the others he said that he would always remain in the service of the king of Spain, and that he would save in his name the cloves left by the Portuguese until the arrival of another of our fleets, and he would never give them to the Portuguese without our consent. He sent as a present to the king of Spain a slave, two *bahars* of cloves (he sent ten, but the ships could not carry them as they were so heavily laden), and two extremely beautiful dead birds.

Those birds are as large as thrushes, and have a small head and a long beak. Their legs are a palm in length and as thin as a reed, and they have no wings, but in their stead long feathers of various colours, like large plumes. Their tail resembles that of the thrush. All the rest of the feathers except the wings are of a tawny colour. They never fly except when there is wind. The people told us that those birds came from the terrestrial paradise, and they call them *bolon diuata*, that is to say, "birds of God."

On that day each one of the kings of the Moluccas

wrote to the king of Spain to say that they desired to be always his true subjects. . . .

Words of those Moorish people:

for their God	Alla
for Christian	naceran
for Turk	rumno
for Moor	musulman; isilam
for Heathen	caphre
for their Mosque	mischit
for Father	bapa
for Mother	mama ambui
for Man	horan
for Woman	poran poan

Pigafetta's complete list contains over 400 words or phrases, is the oldest specimen of the Malay language in existence, and is said to be "wonderfully accurate."

A LEAKY SHIP

As the *Victoria* stood out of the harbour of Tidore, December 18, 1521, the *Trinidad* suddenly began to leak. The desperate efforts of the crew to find the leak were in vain. So were the efforts of Rajah Almanzor's divers, who freed their long hair so that it would be tugged in the direction of the leak by the flow of water into the ship. The *Trinidad* would need a complete overhaul.

But the *Victoria* could not delay if it wished to take advantage of the winter monsoon. This steady seasonal wind, known to Arab and Roman sailors centuries before, began to blow from the north-east in November, and would waft the ship across the Indian Ocean. It was decided that the *Victoria*, commanded by Sebastián del Cano, would sail on.

Some of the *Victoria's* men, however, were so shaken by the near disaster to the *Trinidad* that they chose to stay on Tidore rather than risk their lives on the return voyage. Fifty-four members of the fleet would remain; forty-seven would sail.

On Wednesday morning as we desired to depart from the Moluccas, the king of Tidore, the king of Gilolo, the king of Bachian, and a son of the king of Ternate, all came to accompany us to the island of Mare. The ship *Victoria* set sail, and stood out a little awaiting the ship *Trinidad*. But the latter not being able to weigh anchor, suddenly began to leak in the bottom.

Thereupon, the *Victoria* returned to its anchorage, and we immediately began to lighten the *Trinidad* in order to see whether we could repair it. We found that the water was rushing in as through a pipe, but we were unable to find where it was coming in. All that and the next day we did nothing but work the pump, but we availed nothing.

When our king [Almanzor] heard of it, he came immediately to the ships, and went to considerable trouble in his endeavours to locate the leak. He sent five of his men into the water to see whether they could discover the hole. They remained more than

CAROLVS · VON · GOTS · GNAD · REMISCH ·
KING · ERWELTER · KAISER · KING · ZVO ·
HISSPANIA · VND · BAIDER · SICILEN · ECZ ·
ERCZHERZOG · ZVO · OSTERREICH · HERCZ ·
OG · VON · BVRGVND · BRABANT · ECZ · GRA ·
F · ZVO · FLANDER · TIROL · ECZ · I · ᛫ H · M · D · XX ·

The Emperor Charles V in 1520

one-half hour under water, but were quite unable to find the leak. The king seeing that he could not help us and that the water was increasing hourly, said almost in tears that he would send to the head of the island for three men, who could remain under water a long time.

Our king [Almanzor] came with the three men early on Friday morning. He immediately sent them into the water with their hair hanging loose so that they could locate the leak by that means. They stayed a full hour under water but were quite unable to locate it.

When the king saw that he could be of no assistance, he asked us weeping who of us would go "to Spain to my sovereign, and give him news of me." We replied to him that the *Victoria* would go there in order not to lose the east winds which were beginning to blow, while the other ship until being refitted would await the west winds and would go then to Darién which is located in the other part of the sea in the country of Yucatan.

The king told us that he had two hundred and twenty-five carpenters who would do all the work, and that he would treat all who remained here as his sons. They would not suffer any fatigue beyond two of them to boss the carpenters in their work. He spoke those words so earnestly that he made us all weep.

We of the ship *Victoria*, mistrusting that the ship might open, as it was too heavily laden, lightened it of sixty quintals of cloves, which we had carried into the house where the other cloves were. Some of the men of our ship desired to remain there, as they feared that the ship would not last out the voyage to Spain, but much more for fear lest they perish of hunger.

Later—in April, 1522—the *Trinidad* would attempt the shorter but more difficult trip back to Panama. The secret of avoiding the adverse trade winds on the eastward crossing by sailing at a high northern latitude was not discovered until 1565, however. The *Trinidad* was destined to be driven back to the Moluccas and captured in November, 1522, by the Portuguese, newly arrived on Ternate.

FAREWELL TO THE MOLUCCAS

At last, the *Victoria* weighed anchor. The men embraced and wept at the parting, and bombards were fired. Then Tidore with its steep spice mountain and smoking volcano—its "fiery hill"—fell behind. The ship headed south through shallow seas. It carried letters from the homesick sailors on Tidore and a fortune in cloves.

On the day of St. Thomas, Saturday, December 21, [1521], our king [Almanzor] came to the ships, and assigned us the two pilots whom we had paid to conduct us out of those islands. They said that it was the proper time to leave then, but as our men who stayed behind were writing to Spain, we did not leave until noon.

When that hour came, the ships bid one another

farewell amid the discharge of the cannon, and it seemed as though they were bewailing their last departure. Our men who were to remain accompanied us in their boats a short distance, and then with many tears and embraces we departed.

The king's governor accompanied us as far as the island of Mare. We had no sooner arrived at that island than we bought four praus laden with wood, and in less than one hour we stowed it aboard the ship and then immediately laid our course toward the south-west.

Juan Carvalho stayed [on Tidore]˙with fifty-three of our men, while we comprised forty-seven men and thirteen Indians.

DOUBLING THE CAPE

The *Victoria* took nearly two months passing through the southern island barrier of the East Indies (which number altogether over three thousand islands). At one of these islands, Ombay, the men caulked the ship and Pigafetta discovered natives "[whose] hair [was] raised high up by means of cane combs with long teeth." At another, Timor, he examined fine sandalwood and wax, and learned about demon worship; here a maiden was thrown to sharks and alligators as a sacrifice every year.

A severe storm caused the men to promise a pilgrimage upon their return. Then, on February 11, 1522, the *Victoria* sailed into the "great open sea," the Indian Ocean. Six months of isolation, increasing cold, hunger, and scurvy lay ahead as they veered south of the Portuguese ship lanes and reached the latitude of the cape long before they doubled it.

They sighted Amsterdam Island, which is less than half-way between Australia and the Cape of Good Hope, but could not manage a landing. Several times they had to strike all sails while they attempted repairs on their leaking hull. Lacking salt, their meat spoiled; they were reduced to a diet of rice, and twenty-one men died. Near the Cape of Good Hope the *Victoria* met a Portuguese ship, but, says a Portuguese historian of that time, regretfully, "it did not come into his [the Portuguese captain's] understanding to send her to the bottom".

In spite of some friction, del Cano proved himself a skillful navigator. He and the men resisted the temptation to land at Mozambique, a Portuguese settlement in East Africa, but when they reached the Cape Verde Islands—almost home—they were forced to seek provisions.

On Tuesday night as it drew near Wednesday, February 11, 1522, we left the island of Timor and took to the great open sea called [the Indian Ocean]. Laying our course toward the west south-west, we left the island of Sumatra . . . to the north on our right hand, for fear of the king of Portugal; as well as . . . all the . . . coast of India Major. . . .

In order that we might double the Cape of Good Hope, we descended to forty-two degrees on the side of the Antarctic Pole. We were nine weeks near that cape with our sails hauled down because we had the west and north-west winds on our bow quarter and because of a most furious storm. That cape lies in a latitude of thirty-four and one-half degrees, and is one thousand six hundred leagues from the cape of

Malacca. It is the largest and most dangerous cape in the world.

Some of our men, both sick and well, wished to go to a Portuguese settlement called Mozambique, because the ship was leaking badly, because of the severe cold, and especially because we had no other food than rice and water; for as we had no salt, our provisions of meat had putrefied. Some of the others, however, more desirous of their honour than of their own life, determined to go to Spain living or dead.

Finally by God's help, we doubled that cape on May 6, [1522], at a distance of five leagues. Had we not approached so closely, we could never have doubled it.

Then we sailed north-west for two months continually without taking on any fresh food or water. Twenty-one men died during that short time. When we cast them into the sea, the Christians went to the bottom face upward, while the Indians always went down face downward. Had not God given us good weather we would all have perished of hunger.

Finally, constrained by our great extremity, we went to the islands of Cape Verde. Wednesday, July 9, [1522], we reached one of those islands called Santiago, and immediately sent the boat ashore for food, with the story for the Portuguese that we had lost our foremast under the equinoctial line (although we had lost it upon the Cape of Good Hope), and when we were restepping it, our captain-general had gone to Spain with the other two ships. With those good words and with our merchandise, we got two boatloads of rice.

The Portuguese in the Cape Verde Islands were friendly as long as they believed the Spaniards' story of having come from America. When a sailor showed his spices and the truth leaked out—that the *Victoria* had come from the east, trespassing on the Portuguese zone—the atmosphere changed.

We charged our men when they went ashore in the boat to ask what day it was, and they told us that it was Thursday with the Portuguese. We were greatly surprised for it was Wednesday with us, and we could not see how we had made a mistake; for as I had always kept well, I had set down every day without any interruption. However, as was told us later, it was no error, but as the voyage had been made continually toward the west and we had returned to the same place as does the sun, we had made that gain of twenty-four hours, as is clearly seen.

The boat having returned to the shore again for rice, thirteen men and the boat were detained, because one of them, as we learned afterward in Spain, told the Portuguese that our captain was dead, as well as others, and that we were not going to Spain. Fearing lest we also be taken prisoners by certain caravels, we hastily departed.

The loss of a day, which bewildered Pigafetta, also shocked the survivors because they realized that for at least half the voyage they must have been observing the holy days wrongly, eating meat on Fridays, etc. Peter Martyr, the learned writer at Charles V's court who reported each voyage of discovery as soon as it was completed, gave the correct explanation. Martyr wrote:

"The Spanish fleet, leaving the Cape Verde Islands, proceeded straight to the west, that is to say, it followed the sun, and each day was a little longer than the preceding. . . . Consequently, when the tour of the world was finished—which the sun makes in twenty-four hours from its rising to its setting—the ship had gained an entire day; that is to say, one less than those who remain all that time in the same place."

Magellan's fleet had now shrunk from five ships to one, and from 234 men, or more, to a handful scarcely able to sail that one ship. The 115 who sailed from the Philippines had dwindled to 101 by the time the Moluccas were reached. Then 54 had been left on Tidore. Desertions on Timor, 12 deaths from scurvy on the homeward passage, and the seizure of 13 men by the Portuguese completed the shrinking process.

THE *VICTORIA* COMES HOME

On Saturday, September 6, 1522, we entered the bay of San Lúcar with only eighteen men and the majority of them sick, all that were left of the sixty men who left the Moluccas. Some died of hunger; some deserted at the island of Timor; and some were put to death for crimes.

From that time we left that bay of San Lúcar until the present day of our return, we had sailed fourteen thousand four hundred and sixty leagues, and furthermore had completed the circumnavigation of the world from east to west.

On Monday, September 8, we cast anchor near the quay of Seville, and discharged all our artillery. Tuesday, we all went in shirts and barefoot, each holding a candle, to visit the shrine of Santa Maria de la Victoria, and that of Santa Maria de la Antigua.

Leaving Seville, I went to Valladolid, where I presented to his sacred Majesty, Charles V, neither gold nor silver, but things very highly esteemed by such a sovereign. Among other things I gave him a book, written by my hand, concerning all the matters that had occurred from day to day during our voyage.

The "book" Pigafetta gave Charles V was either a copy of his day-to-day journal, now lost, or merely an oral account of the voyage. Later he wrote the more finished version we are reading.

I left there as best I could and went to Portugal where I spoke with King John III of what I had seen. Passing through Spain, I went to France where I made a gift of certain things from the other hemisphere to the mother of the most Christian king, Francis I, Madame the regent. Then I came to Italy, where I established my permanent abode, and devoted my poor labours to the famous and most illustrious lord, Philippe Villiers l'Ile-Adam, the most worthy grand master of Rhodes.

The Cavalier
Antonio Pigafetta

EPILOGUE

As Pigafetta went from court to court telling the story of the voyage, and as the first accounts were published, Europe applauded Magellan and his men.

"Worthier, indeed, are our sailors of eternal fame than the Argonauts who sailed with Jason," exclaimed Maximilian of Transylvania in 1523. "And much more worthy was their ship of being placed among the stars than that old *Argo;* for that only sailed from Greece through the Black Sea, but ours from Seville to the south; and after that, through the whole west and the southern hemisphere, penetrating into the east, and again returned to the west."

Peter Martyr, who gave the name "New World" to the Americas, agreed. "Children in the primary schools learn the distance that separates Greece from the Black Sea," he wrote. "It is less than the fingernail of a giant!" But Magellan had found "another route leading to the Golden Chersonesus"—that is, the Malay peninsula—and his men had "made the circuit of the globe," an "incredible feat." Many other writers compared Magellan's men to the Argonauts.

Although the Portuguese denounced Magellan as a traitor and Bishop Fonseca's disloyal Spanish officers accused him of highhanded conduct, the facts spoke for themselves. The *Victoria* had been away nearly three years on a voyage of over forty thousand miles. Magellan had found the passage from West to East, had brought Spain into the contest for the Moluccas, and had discovered the magnificent Philippine archipelago, which Spain would hold for three centuries. The Christian faith he planted there is still strong. He had supplied incontrovertible proof that the earth is round and had revealed, for the first time, the extent of the Pacific, greatest of oceans. The next Spanish expedition to the Moluccas, lacking his leadership, failed dismally.

The first landing of Europeans in the Western Hemisphere is obscured in the mists of the past— Norsemen, Portuguese and others as well as Columbus being given credit for making it. But about the first circumnavigation of the globe there is no contention. To one ship and to one man, pre-eminently, belongs the glory.

The ship is the *Victoria*. The man is Ferdinand Magellan, whose determination carried his crew, through unknown straits and seas, around the world.

A TIMETABLE OF EVENTS

March 25, 1505   Magellan sails as gentleman volunteer under Almeida, in Portuguese fleet for East.

July, 1505–
September, 1507   Is stationed at Kilwa, Tanganyika; patrols east African coast against Arab smugglers.

October, 1507   Arrives in Cochin, India; begins duty on Portuguese caravel in Indian Ocean.

February 2, 1509   Fights and is seriously wounded in Battle of Diu, crucial Portuguese naval victory over Egyptians and Arabs.

September, 1509   Helps Portuguese fleet of Sequeira escape Malay trap at Malacca; rescues cousin Francisco Serrano.

January–February,
1510   Starts back to Portugal, but is shipwrecked on the Shoals of Padua in Indian Ocean.

July–August, 1511   Fights at capture of Malacca, Portuguese victory leading to control of East Indies.

1512   Takes his caravel on a mysterious exploring voyage east of Malacca, possibly to Philippines.

1513   Returns to Lisbon, Portugal.

March, 1514   Is wounded in knee and lamed for life fighting in Portuguese expeditionary force in Morocco.

Late 1515 or
early 1516   Is refused permission to sail to the Spice Islands by King Manuel; leaves Lisbon in disgrace.

October 20, 1517   Arrives in Seville, Spain, to present plan for westward voyage to Spice Islands to Charles I.

December, 1517   Marries Lady Beatriz Barbosa, daughter of the governor of the Castle of Seville.

March 22, 1518   Signs contract with King Charles I of Spain for westward voyage to Spice Islands.

October 22, 1518   Receives minor wound in dock riot instigated by Portuguese consul, Alvarez, but saves his flagship from rioters.

August 10, 1519   Sails with fleet from Seville to San Lúcar, on the coast.

September 20, 1519   Departs from San Lúcar, Spain, for westward passage to Spice Islands.

September 27, 1519   Receives warning in Canary Islands of plot to replace him as captain-general with Cartagena.

December 13, 1519   Arrives at Rio de Janeiro, first port of call in New World; gives crews thirteen-day rest.

January 11, 1520   Arrives at Rio de la Plata estuary; is bitterly disappointed to find that it is not the strait he is seeking.

April 1–2, 1520 Puts down mutiny of Cartagena and other Spanish captains in St. Julian, Argentina; punishes the guilty.

May 22, 1520 Loses the *Santiago*, which is wrecked on an exploring voyage off Santa Cruz River.

August 24, 1520 Changes winter quarters from St. Julian to Santa Cruz River, farther south.

October 21, 1520 Arrives at Cape of the Virgins and enters the Strait of Magellan.

November, 1520 Loses the *San Antonio*, which deserts and returns to Spain.

November 28, 1520 Leaves the Strait of Magellan and enters the Pacific Ocean.

March 6, 1521 Arrives at Guam after a three-month voyage across the Pacific.

March 16, 1521 Discovers the Philippine Islands; sights southern cape of Samar.

April 7, 1521 Arrives at Cebu, chief inhabited isle of the Philippines; begins trade and conversion of natives to Christianity.

April 27, 1521 Is killed in the Battle of Mactan, in Philippines, while covering his men's retreat.

May 1, 1521 Many more Spaniards are slain by treachery of natives at a banquet in Philippines.

May, 1521   The *Concepción*, leaking badly, is burned off the Island of Bohol, in Philippines.

November 8, 1521   The fleet, now consisting of *Victoria* and *Trinidad*, arrives in Spice Islands twenty-seven months after leaving Spain.

December 21, 1521   The *Victoria*, with valuable load of spices, sails from Spice Islands for Spain.

May 6, 1522   The *Victoria* doubles the Cape of Good Hope.

September 6, 1522   The *Victoria* arrives at San Lúcar, Spain, having sailed around the world.

INDEX

Abreu, Antonio de, 155
Aden, xxvii
Africa, circled by Portuguese, xviii
Albo, Francisco, log-book, 25, 51, 73, 99, 141, 163
Albuquerque, Alonso de, xxvii, xxviii, xxix, 38
Alexander VI, Pope of Rome, xvi, 3, 4; *see also* Tordesillas, Treaty of
Alexander the Great, xvi
Almagest, xvii
Almanzor, king of Tidore, 151, 154–155, 157, 158–162, 165–169, 171
Almeida, Francisco de, xx–xxi, xxii–xxiii, xxvii, xxix, xxxii
Alvarez, Dom Sebastian, xxxiii, xxxv, xxxvi, 15–20, 71
Amsterdam Island, 173
Antarctic Circle, 75
Antarctic Pole, 55, 56, 80, 92
Arabs, xx, xxi, xxii–xxiii, 30, 115, 157
Argentina, 9, 55, 63
Aristotle, xvi–xvii
Astrolabe, xviii, xix
Atlantic Ocean, 39
Azamor, xxx
Azores, xvii

Bachian, 150, 157, 158, 159, 165, 166, 168
Bahar measure, 160
Barbosa, Doña Beatriz (wife of Magellan), xxxiii, xxxvi, 20, 21, 22–23, 138
Barbosa, Diogo, xxxii, xxxiii
Barbosa, Duarte, xxxiv, 60, 81, 138, 143
Battle of Diu, xxii–xxiii
Battle of Mactan, 130–137
Behaim, Martin, 8–9, 76, 78, 86; globe, 10
Betel nuts, 114
Boii, 43
Borneo, 144–149

Brazil, xii, xvi, 3, 19, 25, 39; discovery of, xxi; natives, 41–49
Brazilwood, 41
Brunei, 144–149
Bulaia, 129, 130

Cabot, Sebastian, 53
Cabral, xxi
Caliban, 70
Calicut, 117
Camoëns, 1
Camphor, 149
Cananore, xxii
Canary Islands, xvii, 38–39, 92
Cannibalism, 42, 46, 53–54, 95
Cano, Sebastián del, 56, 58, 149, 168, 173
Cape Cattigara, 91, 92, 93
Cape Deseado, 79
Cape of the Eleven Thousand Virgins, 73, 91
Cape Frio, 19
Cape of Good Hope, xviii, xx, 75, 82, 173–174
Cape Roque, 39
Cape Saint Mary, 12
Cape St. Vincent, 163
Cape Verde, xvii, 40
Cape Verde Islands, 3, 173, 174–175, 176
Caravels, 30
Cartagena, Juan de, xxxiv, 16, 19, 38, 39–40, 56, 57, 58, 59, 62, 75, 81
Carvalho, Juan, 19, 46, 69, 139–140, 143, 148, 149, 172
Cebu, 99, 114–124
Ceylon, xxii
Channel of All Saints, 82
Charles I, king of Spain (later Charles V), xi–xiv, xxxii, xxxiii, xxxiv, xxxv, xxxvi, 4, 5, 6, 7, 8, 12–15, 27, 29, 83, 101, 112, 155, 156, 160, 162, 165, 176, 177
Charles V. *See* Charles I

Cheleulle, 70
Chièvres, 12
Christian religion, 111–114, 118–124, 127–129, 179
Cilapulapu, king of Mactan, 129, 130–131, 137
Cloves, 157–158
Coca, Captain de, 56
Cochin, xxii
Colambu, king of Limasaua, 106, 107–111, 112–114, 118, 119
Columbus, Christopher, xv, xvi
Compass, xviii; variation of, 92–93
Concepción, xxxvi, 30, 56, 57, 62, 77, 78, 79, 86, 89; burning of, 143
Coria, 36
Corrêa, 38–39, 58–62
Cortereal brothers, 16, 20
Cross-staff, xviii, xix

Darién, 169
De Moluccis Insulis, 4–8
Decades of the New World, 70
Diaz, Bartholomew, xviii
Diu, Battle of, xxii–xxiii

Earth, circumference, xii–xiii, xvii; sphericity, xvi–xvii
Eden, Richard, 70
Egyptians, xxi, xxii–xxiii
Enrique de Malacca, 20, 22, 106, 109, 137–139
Equator, xviii, 93
Eratosthenes, xvii
Espinosa, Gomez de, 57, 59–60, 139, 143, 149

Faleiro, Ruy, xxxi–xxxiii, xxxv, 13, 15, 16, 18, 19
Farol, 31, 32
Ferdinand and Isabella, 3
The First Voyage Around the World, 125
Florida, 87
Flying fish, 87
Fonseca, Bishop Juan Rodriguez de, xi, xiii–xiv, xxxiv, 12, 13, 15, 17, 57, 92, 178
Francis I, king of France, 177

Gama, Vasco da, xx, xxvii, xxxii, 20, 115
Geographia, xvii, xviii
Gilolo, king of, 168
Goa, xxvii
Gomes, Estevan, xxxiv, 75, 78, 80
Greece, ancient, xvi–xvii
Guadalquivir River, xxxvi, 36
Guam, 93–97
Guanacos, 62, 63, 64, 65, 67
Guaraní Indians, 41–49

Hamacas, 43
Haro, Cristóbal de, xi, xiii–xiv, xxxv, xxxvi, 5–6, 7, 9, 16
Henry, Count of Burgundy, xv
Historia de las Indias, 9, 12
Hocem, Mir, xxiii
Homonhon, 105
House of Trade of the Indies, 39
Humabon, king of Cebu, 115–124, 127, 129, 130, 131, 136, 137, 138–139, 143, 158

India, xx, xxii, 5
India House, Lisbon, xxix
Indian Ocean, xvii, xviii, xxii–xxiii, xxvi, 172, 173
Inca Empire, Peru, 53
Indians, Brazil, 41–49; captive, 67–70, 90; Patagonia, 62–70, 87–89; Tierra del Fuego, 86
Indies, Supreme Council of the, xi
Isleo River, 80, 82

John II, king of Portugal, xvi
John III, king of Portugal, 177
Juan Gigante (John the Giant), 65–67

Kilwa, Tanganyika, xxi–xxii
Knights of Rhodes, 27, 28
Knights of Santiago, 83

La Plata River, 9, 12, 53–54, 56
Ladrones, Isles de los (Mariana Islands), 93–97
Las Casas, Bartolomé de, 8, 9, 12
Lateen sails, 30

Legaspi, 122
Lendas da India, 38, 58–62
Leonora, queen of Portugal, xv
Leyte Gulf, 101
Limasaua, 106, 107–108, 109, 114, 118, 119
Line of Demarcation, xii, xvi, 3, 4; *see also* Tordesillas, Treaty of
Lisbon, xv–xvi, xxix
Lloriaga, Captain, 57
Longitude, determination of, xxxii
Longitude zero, 92
Longitudes and latitudes, concept of, xviii–xix
Lusiads, 1

Mactan, 99, 129
Mactan, Battle of, 130–137
Madeiras, xvii
Magellan, Diogo, xv, xx
Magellan, Ferdinand, birth, xiv; character, 136–137; circumnavigation of the earth, 101; death, 133, 136; departure from Seville, xxxv, 33, from San Lúca, xxxvi, 37; early voyages, xx–xxx; family background, xiv–xv; marriage, xxxiii; Order of the Day, 81, 82; will, 20–23; *see also* Charles I; Magellanic clouds; Montevideo; Pacific Ocean; Patagonians; Philippine Islands; Strait of Magellan
Magellan, Isabel, xv
Magellan, Rodrigo, xxxiii, xxxvi, 20, 22
Magellan, Strait of, xiv, 73–89
Magellan Tower, xv
Magellanic clouds, 91, 92
Makian, 150
Malacca, xxiii, xxvii, 5, 6, 101, 117, 150; capture of, xxviii
Malay Peninsula, xxiii, 5, 178; language, 106; word list, 167
Malta, 28
Mamelukes, xxiii
Manuel, king of Portugal, xx, xxvii, xxix, xxx–xxxi, xxxiii, 5, 6, 9, 15–20, 39, 156
Mare, 141, 158, 166, 168, 172
Marine Department, Portugal, xx
Martyr, Peter, 176, 178

Master Andrew, xxxv
Maximilian of Transylvania, 3, 4–8, 83, 86, 165, 178
Mendoza, Luís de, 56, 57, 59–60, 62, 81
Mesquita, Alvaro de, 19, 57, 58, 62, 79
Middle Ages, xvii
Missiglioni, 72
Mohammed, Sultan, xxvi
Mohammedanism, 150
Moluccas (Spice Islands), xii–xiii, xxix, xxx, xxxii, xxxiii, xxxvi, 3–4, 6, 8, 9, 19, 29, 53, 71, 75, 82, 91, 112, 149–162, 165, 171, 178, 179; *see also* Bachian, Mare, Makian, Ternate, Tidore
Monte de Christo, 72
Monte Rosso, 37
Montevideo, 53
Moors, xv, 20, 21
Morocco, xxx
Mortier, 150
Mozambique, 173, 174
Mutiny, St. Julian, 56–62

Naos, 30
Navigation, xviii–xix, 92–93
"New World," xi–xiv, 4–12; name, 178; *see also* Behaim, Martin; Charles I; Columbus, Christopher; Schöner, Johann; Vespucci, Amerigo
Newfoundland, 7
Niña, xvi, 30
North Pole, xviii
Nostra Dona de Barrameda, 37

Ombay, 172
Oporto, xxxi–xxxiii
Ormuz, xxvii

Pacific Ocean, xiv, 8, 89–91, 179
Palawan, 143
Parallel sailing, 92; *see also* Navigation
Patagonian Indians, 62–70, 87–89
Penguins, 54, 55
"Pepperbags," xx
Philip II, king of Spain, 101

Philippine Islands, xxix, 91–92, 101–124, 127–140, 178–179
Pigafetta, Antonio, xxxv, 27–29, 31–37, 39, 40–49, 53–56, 58, 62, 63–72, 75, 82, 83, 86–97, 102–124, 127–140, 143–162, 165–178
Ponte da Barca estate, xv
Port St. Mary, 149
Portuguese, early voyages, xvii–xviii
Ptolemy, xvii, xviii

Quesada, Gasper de, 19, 56, 57, 60, 62, 81

Reina, Pero Sanchez de, 81
Religion, 111–114, 118–124, 127–129, 150, 179
Rio de Janeiro, 41
Rio de Janeiro Bay, 25
Robertson, James A., 28
Ryukyu Islands, 92

St. Elmo's Fire, 39, 41, 56
St. James, 27–28
St. Julian, mutiny at, 56–62
St. Vincent, Cape of, 36
San Antonio, xxxvi, 30, 56, 57, 58, 60, 62, 76, 78–81, 86, 109
San Juan de Aznalfarache, 36
San Lúcar, xxxvi, 36, 37, 176
San Martín, Andrés de, 82, 139
Santa Cruz River, 71, 75
Santa Maria, 30
Santiago (ship), xxxvi, 30, 53, 57, 58; wreck of, 70–72, 75
Santiago Island, 174
Sardine River, 79, 80
Schöner, Johann, 9; globe, 11
Scurvy, 89, 90, 101–102, 109, 172, 176
Seals, 54, 55
Sequeira, Captain, xxiii, xxvi
Serrano, Francisco, xv, xx, xxvi, xxix–xxx, xxxiv, 112, 150, 155–156
Serrano, Juan, xxxiv, 57, 58, 71, 79, 112, 138, 139–140, 143
Setebos, 68, 70
Seville, xxxii–xxxvi
Shakespeare, 70
Siaui, Rajah, 111

Sierra Leone, 40
Solis, Juan de, 9, 53, 54
South America, 7, 8
South China Sea, 5
South Pole, xviii; see also Antarctic Pole
Southern Cross, 93
Sparto rope, 32
Spice Islands. See Moluccas
Spice trade, xiii, xx, xxvii–xxviii, 6, 160–162; see also Cloves
Strait of Magellan, xiv, 73–89
Sumatra, 5, 173
Supreme Council of the Indies, xi

Tagus River, xv, xx, xxix
The Tempest, 70
Tenerife, 37
Ternate, xxx, 1, 150, 155, 156, 168
Tiburoni, 40–41
Tidore, 1, 141, 150, 151–155, 156, 165, 167, 168, 171
Tierra del Fuego, 83–86
Timor, 172, 173
Tordesillas, Treaty of (1494), xii, xvi, 3, 4
Trinidad, xxxiii, xxxvi, 27, 30, 57, 77, 79, 86, 89, 143, 149, 167, 168–169, 171
Turks, 28

Unfortunate Isles, 91

Valderrama, Father, 118
Valladolid, xi, 8
Venice, xxi, xxiii
Vespucci, Amerigo, xiv
Victoria, xxxvi, 27, 30, 56–60, 77, 79–81, 86, 89, 143, 149, 160, 167–171, 172–173, 175–179
Villiers l'Ile-Adam, Philippe, 28, 178

Word lists, Brazilian Indians, 48–49; Malay language, 167; Patagonian Indians, 87–88

Zero longitude, 92
Zula, 130